Scratch My Back

A Pictorial History of the Musical Saw and How to Play It

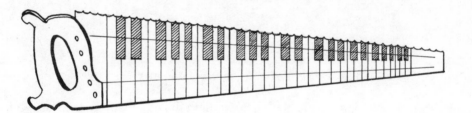

by

Jim "Supersaw" Leonard
and Janet E. Graebner

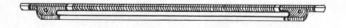

Illustrations by Suzy with a Y

Kaleidoscope Press
Santa Ana, California

This book is produced in cooperation with Seada Records,
P.O. Box 2183, Santa Ana, California 92707

Library of Congress Catalog Card Number 88-82301

ISBN 0-9620882-0-X

Design: Rebecca J. Thompson/Thompson & Thompson
Printing Representative: Jim Mantych/Graphic Masters
Halftones: Prep Graphics

Kaleidoscope Press
1601 West MacArthur – 12F, Santa Ana, California 92704

Printed in the United States of America

To Clarence Mussehl and Dan Wallace

*For their sawnsational efforts to preserve the art of
musical sawing*

Table of Contents

Foreword I

Within these pages is everything you would ever want to know about the musical saw, and much, much more. You will meet sawyers (those who play the instrument) from Maine to California, as well as sawyers from throughout the world; like South American Moses E. Josiah (a Guyanan who gave a special performance on the musical saw for the Queen of England . . . Fitch Cooper, who imitates windstorms and hoot owls . . . Clarence J. Mussehl, the founder of Mussehl & Westphal, the first —and still thriving —professional musical saw company.

Meet crusty Thomas Jefferson Scribner (whom I met in 1981, the same year I "talked saw" with Dan Wallace), the legendary lumberjack who played so well the people of Santa Cruz, California, erected a life-size bronze statue showing him hunched over, playing the traditional woodcutter's tool.

You will be introduced to these and numerous other memorable maestros of the sonorous blade in *Scratch My Back*; a book, incidentally, whose title is a story in itself, about a fiddle playin' lumberjack with an itchy saw.

It's fitting that when co-author Jim "Supersaw" Leonard isn't cutting musical saw tapes (Super Saw, Scratch My Back, and Cookbook), or making personal appearances on radio, television and stage, that he is working as a self-employed gas appliance repairman, because sawyers come from all walks of life. One of my tennis partners, for example, dentist Marty Herzstein, is an accomplished sawyer. In the book, among others, you'll learn that Tatsuo Hamano is a marine biologist and well-known sawyer in Japan; that Australian tree surgeon Larry Hanley uses the saw in his work and play; and that Margaret Steinbuch traded her violin for a saw and played it with the Cincinnati Philharmonic.

Master sawyer Jim "Supersaw" Leonard and his co-author, Janet E. Graebner, take the reader on an enlightening, fascinating and delightful journey to the little-known world of the haunting music of a folk instrument that traces its beginnings to the mid-1800s, in the hills and hollers of Appalachia.

Scratch My Back: A Pictorial History of the Musical Saw and How to Play It is the first book ever published about the carpenter's tool that became a musical instrument. And it's a dandy, as you shall see as you read on.

CHARLES HILLINGER, Columnist, Charles Hillinger's America
Los Angeles Times-Washington Post News Service

Foreword II

The first time I heard the musical saw I was truly amazed. Not so much by the novelty of it, but more by the idea that an instrument with such musical potential had been kept a secret from the masses for so long.

The saw is capable of producing many kinds of sounds and effects, and literally turning a melody into a beautiful listening experience. It can be eerie. It can be comical or dramatic . . . happy or sad. Furthermore, the saw is suited to play virtually any style of music, including folk, rock, country, jazz, classical —you name it. Two saws in harmony sound delightful. Four saws doing Bach chorales is even a possibility. This might someday be known as sawcappella.

As for accompaniment, any type of orchestral backup that would work for a solo vocalist or violinist, for example, could accompany a saw. The American Music Medley that I wrote for saw and orchestra —performed in 1985 by the Los Angeles Philharmonic Orchestra, with sawyer Dave Weiss —has the saw accompanied at times by only the string section, at other instances only by brass or woodwinds, and sometimes by the full orchestra. At one point in the medley, the saw even plays in harmony with a solo violin.

(From left) Sawyer David Weiss, Erich Kunzel (guest conductor, Los Angeles Philharmonic, 1985 Hollywood Bowl performance), and Gary Mandell, arranger-orchestrator

Composition

Making music on a saw did not seem particularly strange to me. If you had an orchestra, which included thirty players bowing on the side of a piece of metal —called a saw —and one day someone created new sounds on a box of wood strung with animal gut —named a violin, but which could just as well have been called a cheese slicer —the sawyers might have thought it pretty funny that someone would play a cheese slicer. The fact is, that in the hands of an accomplished sawyer, you realize that the saw is just as valid an instrument as any other, and capable of emitting some truly beautiful music.

To compose or orchestrate for any instrument, you have to know its range: how high or low in pitch it will go. It is important to remember that every musical saw —like the human voice —has its own idiosyncracies. For example, the Stanley Handyman soprano saw that Dave Weiss usually plays has a range similar to a piccolo. Its lowest note is an octave above middle C, and it goes up about two octaves from there. Other saws that he uses, including his tenor Mussehl & Westphal, have a range starting about a fifth lower.

I have never come across a saw in an orchestration book, or in a book on the range of instruments. So, for ease of composing, let's consider the saw a transposed instrument, like the piccolo. This means that the saw's actual sound is an octave above its written note. Calling the saw a transposed instrument makes it easier to write the music and to read it, otherwise many of the saw's notes would appear way above the staff.

Every instrument has its limitations, so if you are composing or arranging for the saw and feel that a passage in the music does not lend itself to the saw's range, let some other instrument carry the melody.

Sounds and Versatility

Aesthetically, I would describe the saw's sound as the blending of a violin, a soprano, and someone whistling; and depending on the register —how high or low in pitch it is played — the saw can "become" more of one of those sounds than another.

Technically, its instrumental capabilities might be described as a combination between a violin and a trombone. Sawyers generally play with a bow, and how much the saw is bent to produce a pitch is analagous to how far trombonists extend their slides. For a trombonist to play notes quickly between a full extension and contraction of the slide is difficult, maybe impossible. Likewise, notes on the musical saw that are played rapidly between a flex from high to low pitch will be difficult to play, but not impossible. [Editor's note: See Chapter 8, Pitch.]

Like other bowed instruments (eventually we might see violin markings for up and down bowing applied to saw music) several notes may be played on the saw with one stroke. This provides smoother phrasing of a group of notes, similar to a woodwind musician playing several notes with one breath. For more definition, however, each note can be bowed individually.

The saw, like other instruments, is capable of sustaining a note, and it also has the capacity for a true glissando: the connecting of two pitches by gliding or sliding between them.

A sawyer's option to apply vibrato offers another attraction, and further indicates the saw's versatility as an instrument. The saw's vibrato is probably closer in sound to that of a guitar or other fretted instrument, rather than a violin.

Probably the musical saw's major shortcoming is its inability to simultaneously produce tones in the bass and treble clef, as in chords. On stringed instruments, more treble is heard the closer you play to the bridge (where the strings attach to the body). As you move farther from the bridge, the bass increases. On a saw, the only way you can change the treble or bass range is by changing saws.

Finally, to my knowledge, the foregoing information is not available in any current music literature. As a composer and arranger, I treat the saw as I would any other instrument, and I hope that most people —whether or not they are involved in playing or composing for the saw —would come to enjoy and recognize its singular sound as that of a legitimate instrument, a designation that the musical saw so rightly deserves.

GARY MANDELL
Los Angeles, California

[Editor's note: See Appendix D.]

International Musical Saw Festival and Saw-Off

From around the world they come. Like bears to a honey pot, sawyers gravitate to a saw festival wherever it is held. In some cases, they will travel thousands of miles to renew old acquaintances, make new friends, and show off what they have learned about the art of musical sawing since the last time they were all together.

Everyone becomes an integral part of the festival because there is always a relaxed, we're-here-to-have-fun camaraderie among sawyers that immediately puts new saw players at ease; and that draws in spectators who are intrigued by the unusual sight and sound. Many of them —just for fun, they say —participate in the musical saw workshops; then a year or two later we see them returning to compete in the saw contest.

In 1987 and 1988 the International Musical Saw Festival and Saw-Off, under the direction of Jim Leonard, was held at California State University, Northridge, in conjunction with Elaine and Clark Weissman's annual Summer Solstice Dulcimer and Traditional Music and Dance Festival. Moses Josiah and David Weiss judged the 1987 saw-off; in 1988, Moses, David, and Steve Porter were the judges.

The following people were winners in the 1987 musical saw contest:

Novelty
1) Doug Cameron, Vancouver, British Columbia
2) Deborah L. McConnaughy, Sylmar, California
3) Dorothy E. Flanagan, Redlands, California

Pop-Jazz
1) Steve F. Porter, Ferndale, California
2) Janeen Rae Heller, Burbank, California
3) Robert N. Froehner, Grand Prairie, Texas

Gospel
1) Virginia C. Davis, Hesperia, California
2) Roland E. Davenport, El Segundo, California
3) Charles W. Hardy, Dearborn Heights, Michigan

Traditional
1) Henry Dagg, Belfast, Northern Ireland
2) Roy K. Thoreson, Calgary, Alberta
3) David B. Hudnut, Tiburon, California

Classical
1) Doug Cameron, Vancouver, British Columbia
2) Dorothy E. Flanagan, Redlands, California
3) Warren R. Hinze, St. Paul, Minnesota

Henry Dagg, a sound engineer with the British Broadcasting Corporation in Belfast, Northern Ireland, was awarded a certificate for traveling the farthest, 5,130 miles, as the crow flies.

Jim Leonard presented Moses Josiah and David Weiss with inscribed gold-plated Mussehl & Westphal saws, in recognition of their Master Sawyer achievements.

Frank Holley, 1987 (Adam Leonard, photographer)

Sean Leonard and Mary Kay Dawson, 1987 (Adam Leonard, photographer)

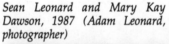

"Signore Antonio Rigatoni" (Doug Cameron); 1987 International Musical Saw Festival and Saw-Off, Northridge, California (Adam Leonard, photographer)

(From left) Moses Josiah, Patricia Graham, and David Weiss, 1987 (Peter Graebner, photographer)

Adam Leonard, sound engineer, 1987 (Jim Leonard, photographer)

(From left) Moses Josiah, Dorothy Flanagan, and David Weiss, 1987 (Peter Graebner, photographer)

John Moran, 1987 (Adam Leonard, photographer)

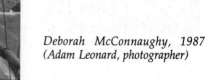

Jim Leonard and Janet E. Graebner, 1987 (Peter Graebner, photographer)

Deborah McConnaughy, 1987 (Adam Leonard, photographer)

Roy Thoreson, 1987 (Adam Leonard, photographer)

Dorothy Flanagan, 1987 (Adam Leonard, photographer)

Virginia C. Davis, 1987 (Adam Leonard, photographer)

The 1988 musical saw contest winners were:

Classical
1) Henry Dagg, Belfast, Northern Ireland
2) Peter Hong, Encino, California
3) Robert N. Froehner, Grand Prairie, Texas

Traditional
1) Frank Holley, Inyokern, California
2) Roy K. Thoreson, Calgary, Alberta
3) Roland Hill, Burbank, California

Gospel
1) Deborah L. McConnaughy, Sylmar, California
2) Debbie Bellante, Killeen, Texas
3) Patricia Graham, Santa Ana, California

Pop-Jazz
1) Henry Dagg, Belfast, Northern Ireland
2) Robert N. Froehner, Grand Prairie, Texas
3) Joe Eding, San Jose, California

Novelty
1) Deborah L. McConnaughy, Sylmar, California
2) Doug Cameron, Vancouver, British Columbia
3) Robert N. Froehner, Grand Prairie, Texas

In recognition of more than sixty years as an old-time sawyer and promoter of the musical saw, the contest judges presented a special award to Ellis Traub of Boca Raton, Florida.

Inscribed gold-plated Mussehl & Westphal saws, recognizing them as Master Sawyers, were awarded to: Doug Cameron, Henry Dagg, and Frank Holley.

(From left) Moses Josiah, David Weiss, Steve Porter, judges at the 1988 International Musical Saw Festival and Saw-Off, Northridge, California

Gold-plated Master Sawyer awards were presented to Frank Holley, Henry Dagg, and Doug Cameron (from left, with saws); (far left) Moses Josiah; (far right) David Weiss; (seated) Jim "Supersaw" Leonard, 1988

Father's Day celebration at the 1988 International Musical Saw Festival; (from left) Adam Leonard, Jim Leonard, Sean Leonard

Jim Wallace, representative for Mussehl & Westphal Professional Musical Saws, 1988 (Jim Leonard, photographer)

Sawing on the Venice boardwalk, (from left) Bob Froehner, Jim Leonard, Moses Josiah, Henry Dagg, Pat Graham, David Weiss, 1988 (David Weiss, photographer)

Venice, California, (from left) Pat Graham, Henry Dagg, Moses Josiah, Jim Leonard, Bob Froehner, 1988 (David Weiss, photographer)

From left: Moses Josiah, Jim Leonard, David Weiss, at the 1988 International Musical Saw Festival and Saw-Off, Northridge, California

I nitially, our intent was simply to preserve a bit of American musical history on a subject that many considered a dying art. Our research proved otherwise. Musical sawing is alive and well. You hold the proof in your hands.

No definitive work has been written on the musical saw. In fact, there is virtually no material on the subject, except for occasional articles on sawyers whenever they appear at local events. *Scratch My Back* is the first attempt by anyone to track the musical saw's history; to discuss the saw's complexity as a vibrating instrument; to present the saw's flexibility; and to recognize the many people —sawyers and non-sawyers —dedicated to preserving the colorful aspects of a not-so-dying art.

Our enthusiasm for writing *Scratch My Back* was heightened by Jim's recent visit to the Weaver family's home near Springfield, Missouri. As popular vaudeville stage and Hollywood screen entertainers during the early part of the twentieth century, the Weavers —Leon, Frank, and June —sawed their way into the hearts of millions, and became our touchstone with the first documented history of the musical saw.

So many people have shared this book with us. We felt truly honored by the immediate and open response from friends and sawyers world-wide who contributed articles, anecdotes, photos, letters, historical and technical information, and —above all —love and encouragement from concept to completion.

A special note of gratitude for a great deal of patience and understanding goes to our illustrator, Suzy Ingram; and to Peter Graebner, for his contributions to the saw's sound production. To all of you, this is your book, and we thank you for helping us write it.

Acknowledgments

French Alain, Hudson Bay, Saskatchewan
William Aleman, Round Hill, Trujillo
    Alto, Puerto Rico
Robert Armstrong, Dixon, California
Jack Arons, Sherman Oaks, California
Grover R. Austad, Great Falls, Montana

Duane L. Beck, Winchester, Indiana
Clifford L. Bedell, Mason, Michigan
Earl J. Beeninga, Monroe, South Dakota
Debbie Bellante, Killeen, Texas
Charlie Blacklock, Alameda, California
René Bogart,* Barre, Massachusetts
Victoria Bolam, Santa Cruz, California
Fred Boldt, North Hollywood, California
Samuel Brignoni, Rio Piedras, Puerto Rico
Henry Brodersen, Niles, Michigan
Jeff Brown, Juneau, Alaska
Georgia Brunner, Springfield, Missouri
Joseph B. Butler, Lee's Summit, Missouri

Doug Cameron, Vancouver, British
    Columbia
Harry J. Cassaly, Westwego, Louisiana
Morgan J. Cowin, San Francisco, California
Clayton Cressman, Quakertown,
    Pennsylvania
Stephen Cseri, Deseronto, Ontario

Henry Dagg, Belfast, Northern Ireland
Roland E. Davenport, El Segundo,
    California
Virginia C. Davis, Hesperia, California
Clyde Dawson,* Anaheim, California
Dave Dawson, Goolwa, South Australia
Louise Dawson, Anaheim, California
Mary Kay Dawson, Delavan, Wisconsin
Allan J. de Lay, Portland, Oregon
McKinley A. DeShield, Jr., Greensboro,
    North Carolina
C. James Dudley, Jr., School of the Ozarks,
    Point Lookout, Missouri

Joel Eckhaus, Brunswick, Maine

Joe Eding, San Jose, California
Joe Emmons, Hillsboro, Ohio
Edmund G. Estrada, Oxnard, California
Harold A. Ezri, Ladoga, Indiana

Kathryn H. Fain, Rosenberg, Texas
Dorothy Jean Farmer, San Jose, California
Dorothy E. Flanagan, Redlands, California
Jim Flowers, Burley, Idaho
Charles B. Foley, San Jose, California
Sarah Foster, Tribune, Kansas
Don Frank, Alexandria, Virginia
E. Charles French, Santa Ana, California
Robert N. Froehner, Grand Prairie, Texas
Gary Froiland, Oakland, Minnesota

L.J. Ganshert, Gratiot, Wisconsin
Burney Garelick, Vista, California
Don Giroux, Santa Clara, California
Allen Givens, Harley, Ontario
William C. Goodman, Melbourne, Florida
Peter Graebner, Santa Ana, California
Patricia Graham, Santa Ana, California

Elfriede Hablé, Vienna, Austria
Phil Hall, Alpine, California
Tatsuo Hamano, Fukuoka, Japan
Larry Hanley, Nambour, Queensland,
    Australia
Charles W. Hardy, Dearborn Heights,
    Michigan
Tobe Heaton, Rancho Palos Verdes,
    California
Bill Heier, San Francisco, California
Janeen Rae Heller, Burbank, California
Martin J. Herzstein, Rancho Palos Verdes,
    California
John Heying,* Orange, California
Roland Hill, Burbank, California
LeRay V. Hinchman, San Jose, California
Warren R. Hinze, St. Paul, Minnesota
Frank Holley, Inyokern, California
Peter Hong, Encino, California
David B. Hudnut, Tiburon, California

Acknowledgments (continued)

John West Hunt, Red Bank, New Jersey
Joe R. Hunter,* Lumsden, Saskatchewan
Larry E. Hunter, Lumsden Saskatchewan
William L. Hunter, Greenville, Tennessee

Suzy Ingram, Ontario, California

Henry Jankiewicz, Syracuse, New York
Betty Johnson, Vista, California
Graham Johnson, Hollywood, California
Spider Johnson, Austin, Texas
Moses E. Josiah, Brooklyn, New York

Kale W. Kaleialii, Sunland, California
Francis R. Kasenda, Limbe, Malawi,
    Africa
Ike W. Kusisto,* Prescott Valley, Arizona

Chuck Larkin, Atlanta, Georgia
Hazel S. Lawson, Battle Creek, Michigan
Barney LeDuc, Long Beach, California
Adam Leonard, Santa Ana, California
Sean Leonard, Santa Ana, California
Debra A. Lindblom, Ontario, California
Wayne Lindblom, Ontario, California
Paul Lovens, Genova, Italy

Len A. MacEachron, St. Paul, Minnesota
George H. Madden, Mount Dora, Florida
Gary Mandell, Los Angeles, California
Bill McClory, Teeswater, Ontario
Deborah L. McConnaughy, Sylmar,
    California
Marian McDermott, Deerfield, Illinois
Henry Menges, Fort Myers, Florida
James P. Meyer, Chicago, Illinois
Jerold S. Meyer, Chicago, Illinois
Philip W. Miner, Santa Ana, California
Utaroku, Miyakoya, Tokyo, Japan
Myrtle Mizell, Vienna, Illinois
David B. Moore, Cambridge,
    Massachusetts
Charles L. Mullen, Cincinnati, Ohio

Grover F. Naylor, Jr., Beeville, Texas
Clark Niederjohn, Los Angeles, California
Charles K. Noyes, New York City,
    New York

Toshitaka Onoe, Yokohama, Japan
William L. Ormandy, Milwaukie, Oregon
Alfred E. Ornehaug, Randolph, New York
Howard T. Orr, Dana Point, California

Ernest W. Peisker, Chicago, Illinois
Davis T. Pillsbury, San Marino, California
Steve Porter, Ferndale, California
Robert C. Pritikin, San Francisco,
    California
Lillian Pullen, Council Bluffs, Iowa

Randy Raine-Reusch, Vancouver, British
    Columbia
Cyril I. Reid, Anaheim, California
Vernon D. Remelin,* Bell, California
Henri H. Repp, Buena Park, California
Emil Richards, Hollywood, California
Ray Ricketts, Fayetteville, Arkansas
Dave Robinson, Northampton,
    Massachusetts

Thomas J. Scribner,* Santa Cruz, California
Si Siman, Springfield, Missouri
Joan F. Snyder, Lancaster, California
Nancy Spencer, Corvallis, Oregon
Margaret Steinbuch,* Cincinnati, Ohio
Earl R. Stuckenbruck, Johnson City,
    Tennessee
Ben Sweeney, Campbell, California

Art Thieme, Peru, Illinois
James A. Thomson, Jr., Locust Grove,
    Georgia
Roy K. Thoreson, Calgary, Alberta
Ellis Traub, Boca Raton, Florida

E. Van der Hoog, The Hague,
    The Netherlands

Acknowledgments (continued)

Vic Vent, Mesa, Arizona
Ben Vinikour, Mount Prospect, Illinois

Al Waeffler,* Monroe, Wisconsin
Carl Wallace, Delavan, Wisconsin
Dan Wallace,* Delavan, Wisconsin
James Winchester Wallace, Delavan, Wisconsin
Charles A. Warren, Pisgah Forest, North
    Carolina

David Weiss, Los Angeles, California
Stan Werbin, Lansing, Michigan
Ray E. Wilhite, Garden Grove, California

Lou Zocchi, Gulfport, Mississippi

* Deceased

The Musical Saw

The saw is a musical darling
It never complains of abuse
It may sing and saw wood the same hour
With never a squawk or excuse.

Now the oboe will whine like a baby
And the bassoon will growl like a bear
The fiddle will squeal for attention
And the trumpet will blatantly blare.

The piano may play only black notes
The string bass will just thump its chest
The drumsticks will clash with the cymbals
And the organ will drown out the rest.

But the saw? It just sits there all mellow
Plays sweet or plays blue —either way
And for kicks, it may stop playing music
And relax and saw wood for a day!

BEN SWEENEY
Campbell, California

PART I

A Philosawphical Overview

C reating a haunting will-o'-the-wisp sound that defies description, the musical saw's eerie trembling tones have been compared alternately to a cat's backfence meowing and a soprano's lyric trill, or to a violin's vibrato and a banshee's wail. Some listeners say the music is willowy and harmonious, while others insist the whistling effect drives every four-footed animal within earshot —and maybe a few two-legged creatures —into the nearest hills.

Daring even otherworldly comparisons, one delightful Paul Bunyan-like tale describes a lumberjack's dream in which his saw stands before him, and —although appreciative of the woodsman's kind handling —complains, "John, my back itches something fierce, and if you'll scratch it for me I'll hum the sweetest music you ever heard this side of heaven."

Whether heavenly or unearthly, the ambivalence surrounding the saw's musicality is only one of several debated questions. For example, is it a tool or an instrument?

Despite guffaws to the contrary, the singing saw is considered an authentic American folk instrument.

But from where?

Some say the Ozarks. From the lips of others: the Appalachians. Still others say musical sawing originated in Scandinavia during the 1800s, or in South America where the natives were known to strike their large crosscut saws to accompany their work songs. It has even been suggested that the musical saw arrived in the United States on the African slave ships of the 1700s.

Actually, no one knows with certainty who discovered that violin-like music could be drawn from the common handsaw, much less when, although general agreement dates it from the mid-nineteenth century, with the saw's greatest popularity spanning the vaudeville circuit during the 1920s and 1930s.

Such contradictions are part of the charm of this unique tool-instrument, illustrating well —lost origins notwithstanding —that the ordinary crosscut or ripsaw has been lifted from the workshed and recognized as more than just a tool for cutting firewood or sawing a two-by-four.

A Musical What?

Recognized, yes. Accepted, no. Group conversations freeze on hearing the words "musical saw." The letters hang in the icy void like the sword of Damocles poised over everyone's head. "Must be a great Halloween joke," someone finally says, referring to the saw's ghostly sighing which resembles the resonance of a glass harmonica or a theremin.

As a musical instrument, the carpenter's saw is still judged a comic fluke by many people, even after they have heard beautiful melodies rendered in the hands of competent sawyers, those who have mastered the tricky business of scratching more than do-re-mi from the backside of the blade with a bow. Skepticism that a handsaw can really make music, or that it is indeed a "real saw" (one that cuts wood), sometimes leads to unexpected situations as performers are challenged to "Cut this board!"

Not always satisfied with such obvious demonstrations, however, some suspicious listeners have required even more from a sawyer, as Martin Larsson found out in Sweden (circa 1917) when saw-goers demanded that he play "Under the Bridges of Paris" with a bun stuck in his mouth! They wanted to make sure the music came from the saw and was not just a clever whistling act.

Groan-producing puns go saw in hand with this particular subject. Did you know, for example, that sawyers play "Flight of the Bumblebee" on buzz saws? Or that musicians who want to imitate an entire orchestra employ band saws? Cab drivers use hack saws, while psychiatrists recommend . . . but you get the idea, so we will cut this short.

Joe Budde, New Orleans, Louisiana, proving that his musical saw can really cut wood (Allan J. de Lay, photographer)

Around the World

What prompts untold numbers —from Oregon to Massachusetts, from Canada to Japan to Australia to Africa, from Borneo to Brazil and other foreign points —to pursue this peculiar musical mutation that generates smirks and raised eyebrows?

For many people it is the pleasure of creating an unusual sound. There is also the glamour associated with being able to actually play such a bizarre instrument. After all, the ability to manipulate musically a wavering sliver of steel (described as high frequency jello by one reporter) is hardly a garden-variety hobby, and many sawyers gladly provide entertainment at the drop of a hint —or without, for that matter.

Despite less than wild public acclaim for the saw's musical properties, enthusiasts' desire to share music, performed on one of the few instruments considered native to this country, spurs them to browse in their basement for a saw with music in it. "We have to drag it out of the dustbin of history," mused Tom Scribner, the legendary sawyer from Santa Cruz, California.

If the comments from our sawyers and correspondents are any indication, that is exactly their intent: to saw life into a dying art and to have fun doing it.

If You Can Hum or Whistle

Who can saw a song? Anyone who can hum, whistle or carry a tune, according to the late Clarence J. Mussehl, the 1921 founder of the world's first —and still thriving —professional musical saw company, Mussehl & Westphal. Aspiring saw players are generally self-taught, and since the musical saw is considered a play-by-ear instrument (no dreary hours of practicing finger exercises!) most beginners, Mussehl always claimed, can learn to play simple tunes the same day they receive their saws.

Scores of letters written to Clarence over five decades from initially dubious would-be sawyers verified the ease with which they learned to play. Notes one correspondent from Winnipeg, Manitoba: "I was delighted to find that you were justified in all you said in your advertisements. In less than a month the saw has been a real money-maker for me. I have played in churches, theatres, hospitals, and every kind of concert hall, and can honestly say the saw has always lined up with the best on the bill."

Another musical handyman, Jerry Lama, sawed his way to success in the 1920s on a Mussehl & Westphal mail order saw, and wrote: "Had it not been for the musical saw I would probably be a common laborer today." Trained on the violin and string bass, Lama put together a novelty act that included his saw and "wind instruments" like the automobile tube, bicycle pump, toy balloons, and rubber gloves. After perfecting his musical sawing technique, Lama also played with the Lehigh Serenaders and the Frank Dennis Orchestra. Dubbed the "Sawing King of the Bronx," Lama capped a distinguished radio career in the late 1930s by appearing —are you ready for this? —on television.

Music is the universal language of mankind, the poet Henry Wadsworth Longfellow said, and sawyers from around the globe penned testimonials that appeared in Clarence Mussehl's annual *Sawing News of the World*, offering proof that in rough hands or smooth —whether a tree surgeon in New Zealand, a missionary in Borneo, or a child in Little Rock —many were tuning their saws to a variety of easy-tempo rhythms like "Annie Laurie," "Smilin' Thru," "My Bonnie Lies Over the Ocean," "Brahm's Cradle Song," "Among My Souvenirs," and "other slow-moving ballads that do not go over an octave and two notes" (Claude N. Ballard in his 1938 publication, *The Musical Saw and How to Play It*).

In general, at the turn of the century, fast-paced songs and classical music appeared to escape interpretation on the humble handsaw, although it is said that in 1928 a German by the name of Kleiber performed a saw solo with the Berlin State Opera.

Breakthrough

If no one was yet experimenting with more than slow songs, neither was anyone coming forth as a composer of saw music. No one, that is, until Louis Gruenberg, who achieved a significant breakthrough for the serious side of sawing on October 17, 1937.

On that date the Columbia Broadcasting System in New York featured Stanley Davis, playing "Rima's Song" in Gruenberg's radio opera *Green Mansions*. The opera (adapted from W.H. Hudson's novel of the same name) recounts the romantic story of Rima, a South American jungle girl, and Abel, an explorer. With "Rima's Song" destined for the saw, Gruenberg became (as far as anyone knows) the first composer to write for what many considered an utterly impossible excuse for a musical instrument.

Referring to *Green Mansions* in her article, "The Apotheosis of the Saw," for the *New Yorker* (May 7, 1938), Lucille Fletcher said that Rima's "voice," calling to Abel in a language taught to her by the birds, captivated the audience and created a memorable day in the history of music. Unquestionably, the saw had been elevated from its backwoods reputation as a novelty item, but few musicians during the musical saw's early days in the United States bothered to explore its symphonic potential. Hence, Fletcher's prediction that the saw would become an accepted orchestral instrument did not, unfortunately, come true.

La Lame sonore

In France, however, a different story emerged concerning the saw's classic pretensions. The French *lame sonore* (the sonorous blade) was, unlike the handsaw, smooth on both sides and it had a lever with finger rests attached at the tip, supposedly for achieving better control while bending the blade, thus allowing the sawyer to produce more precise tones. (Many saw purists eschew such accessories as levers or tip-end grips and develop very strong fingers to manipulate the blade.)

This toothless "saw" is documented in a study by French musicologist Jacques Keller, who cites as its predecessor the more rustic woodsman's tool hammered for entertainment in the Argentine logging camps of the 1800s. Noting from his late 1940s perspective that the musical saw "enjoyed a lively but brief popularity thirty years ago," Keller credits Claude Duboscq with "transforming the very soul of this metal, so [incredibly] musical." Duboscq, says Keller, used the *lame sonore* as a concert instrument, in theatrical productions, and as accompaniment for choral groups.

Compositions by Bach, Handel, Wagner and others are transposed for the saw and included in Keller's book, along with original saw arrangements by composers Duboscq, Charles Koechlin, Henri Sauguet, and Dom Clement Jacob, among others. (In America, after the 1940s, a clique of composers and performers also began including the musical saw in some of their works, most notably: Aram Khatchaturian, Hans Werner Henze, Arthur Honegger, David Burge, and jazz musician Dave Brubeck.)

Illustrating the French tendency to rhapsodize, Keller exclaims, "[The saw's] magical voice [is] unlike anything else. It's absolutely enchanting to hear such moving sonority, the more so because it sounds so human. Why would anyone want to confine it to the circus or music hall?"

Why indeed, and as we examine the musical saw's history in the following pages it will become clear that others, too, envisioned it as more than "just an old saw."

Saw of Ages

As one of the oldest tools known to man (probably evolving from jagged rocks) the saw has been tempered to the times. Artisans have always tried to improve on the efficiency of the tool, whether manufacturing blades from flint (circa 8000 B.C), or from copper or bronze (circa 3000 B.C.). The Iron Age saw significantly improved blades, but it was only after the invention of steel by the Chalybes, about 1400 B.C., that carefully shaped and tapered saws with set teeth could be produced.

As a descendent of those earlier achievements, the musical saw has also undergone change and has transcended —not in every sawyer's opinion, mind you —its beginnings as a workman's tool. Since only about one in a hundred handsaws are musically inclined (depending on the quality of the steel, its flexibility, and the symmetry between length and width) many of the first saw hopefuls experienced great frustration at not getting more than a dull thunk out of their cellar saws. Even among those who managed to hammer out a respectable "Ah! Sweet Mystery of Life," no one —yet —had forged beyond the handsaw's one-octave range.

A Sawnsational Accident

Enter Clarence Mussehl, who, in 1919, accidentally came across the musical saw during a vaudeville show at Milwaukee, Wisconsin's old Majestic Theatre. Most of the show was forgettable, but a novelty act billed as the Weaver Brothers featured Leon Weaver playing a carpenter's saw, and Clarence was fascinated enough to later spend his life mastering its secrets and promoting what he considered an often maligned and little understood instrument.

Destiny must have arranged Mussehl's chance viewing of the Weaver Brothers' act, for it was Leon Weaver who, fifteen years earlier, in the grip of his own fascination with the saw, had hammered his way to fame, thus providing us with the first known recorded history of this unusual folk instrument.

Now Clarence, sharpening his own reputation as well as extending the saw's versatility, arrived to achieve a remarkable first by developing a professional musical saw that was cut from softer English steel. It was longer, thinner, and more flexible, thereby offering a greater range and volume than the one-octave (if you could find it) carpenter's saw. Mussehl's refinement of the instrument created a controversy among sawyers —still unresolved —in which one side insisted that any store-bought saw would sing, and the other side claimed that only a blade ground to rigid specifications would intone saw-worthy notes.

How fortunate that Leon and Clarence came together, for although neither invented the musical saw, it is doubtful that we would be enjoying its haunting will-o'-the-wisp sound today without their efforts. Still making the sweetest music this side of heaven when a sawyer scratches its back, the saw's proven adaptability as a musical instrument continues to captivate audiences everywhere.

Windstorms and Hoot Owls

Imagine a vaudeville performer named Leon Weaver and put him in Springfield, Missouri, 1904. Add a chance meeting with a man from the Ozarks, one Fitch Cooper, who was imitating windstorms and hoot owls with a club on a carpenter's saw. Hear Opportunity knock as Leon realizes that manipulation of the saw could be extended beyond hoots and howls to a higher musical art form.

Leon Weaver is our touchstone with the first documented history on the musical saw. There is general agreement among sawyers and sawficionados that the musical saw's origins date from about the mid-1800s, in the eastern mountains of the United States. In keeping with the notion that the singing saw may have been born in the hands of mountain musicians, a story is told of an itinerant Appalachian printer, known only as Slim, who used to show up at weddings and other festive events, saw in hand. After entertaining the merrymakers, Slim would fill up on as much free food and drink as possible before wending his way elsewhere. He was last reported to have made an appearance in Springfield, Missouri, around the turn of the century.

But although the sonorous blade fits in well with other mountain music instruments — like the banjo, bazooka, jugs, washboards, and spoons, to name only a few —no one really knows who discovered that music could be coaxed from the flat side of a tapered straightback saw. Quite possibly its world-wide popularity surfaced simultaneously in several places as merchants, missionaries, travelers, and immigrants circled the globe. Lou Zocchi, for example, a magician-sawyer from Gulfport, Mississippi, recalls hearing that the saw was brought to America by a German immigrant shortly after the American Civil War (1861-65). Others mention their surprise, while traveling, in finding the musical saw played by missionaries in such remote places as Borneo, Brazil, and Malaya.

Placing the saw's appearance even earlier than the 1850s, however, the left-handed sawyer known as "Diversified Doc" (Dr. McKinley DeShield, Jr., born in Liberia, West Africa

and now living in Greensboro, North Carolina) suggests the whispering foil could have been introduced in the United States with the import of African slaves during the eighteenth century. Then, as now, DeShield says, African villagers used to scrape on handsaws to make music during ceremonial dances.

Legends and speculation aside, the saw's musical origins— like its unusual sound that escapes precise definition —elude verification, and it is for this reason that Leon Weaver's efforts, commencing in 1904, become historically important.

Lou Zocchi, sawyer, ventriloquist, and magician

Practice Makes Perfect

practice, Practice, PRACTICE! say sawyers, and that is what Leon did for two years, pounding out melodies with a padded hammer as he had seen Fitch Cooper do.

Finally, he felt sufficiently accomplished to embark on a tour through Missouri, Texas, and Arkansas with Dr. A.B. Christie's traveling medicine show. He was a sensational success, providing musical entertainment while Dr. Christie peddled his magic elixir for a dollar a bottle.

Despite his popularity, Leon could not overcome the public's skepticism that the humming saw was just a gimmick. After every performance he had to prove that his musical wood cutter could indeed sink its teeth into a plank as well as hammer out a tune.

Such "show me" demonstrations are still part of the fun, Massachusetts sawyer René Bogart says, recalling a performance with his Les Jardienne Trio, when a carpenter in the audience scoffed, "That's not a real saw!"

"It's not? You just keep watching," René retorted, as he began to saw the legs off the wooden chair he had just been sitting on.

René generally uses a cello bow to stroke his saw, but occasionally he substitutes a coat hanger or a cane. You will not, however, catch him with a mallet in his hand like Leon Weaver used. "GOD FORBID!" René writes. "I NEVER HAMMER A MUSICAL INSTRUMENT!"

The Weavers

The Weaver Brothers and Elviry, Ralph Foster Museum, School of the Ozarks, Point Lookout, Missouri (Jim Leonard, photographer)
From left: "Abner" (Leon) 1882-1950; "Elviry" (June) 1891-1977; "Cicero" (Frank) 1891-1967
Bas-relief legend: Ozarks born and reared, [the] Weaver Brothers and Elviry presented one of the greatest stage attractions ever to tour the United States and Canada. Great enough to be booked by the famed Morris Agency of New York. They were acclaimed by critics and were much in demand for return engagements wherever they appeared. They performed before the crowned heads of Europe. Their unique country-style of music and rural humor delighted people in all walks of life. They were truly the forerunners of the popularity of country music "pickin' and singin'" today! The entire Weaver family were gifted musicians and had a natural flair for entertaining. They sang and played in schoolhouses, halls and churches all over the Ozarks before being "discovered" by the largest and finest theatres in the nation—including a two weeks' run at the famed Palace Theatre in New York City, the ultimate goal of all show people! The contribution to the traditions and folklore of the Ozarks is inestimable. Their place in the Ozarks Hall of Fame is richly deserved!

Unlike René, however —who says he had heard "some German fellow play the saw about 1910 at the Elmwood Music Hall in Buffalo, New York" —Leon had no model sawyer to copy. Trial and Error were his teachers. They were, that is, until sister-in-law June Weaver came along. June (Frank's wife) was not only an accomplished musician but also a determined woman. More important, she had a streak of curiosity that led to several innovations that dramatically reformed the art of musical sawing for all time.

During the decade that Leon worked the vaudeville circuit alone, June and Frank fooled with the saw off and on, and by 1916 they had achieved enough sawbility to join Leon on stage. But there was a slight hitch. They held the saw the way Leon had seen Fitch Cooper play it: sitting on the handle with his legs spread, the blade extended forward. Considered unladylike for June, this spread-eagle position prevented her from playing in public. Fretfully, she scratched second fiddle (figuratively speaking; actually she played the rake, autoharp, and bicycle pump) while the men received all the attention.

Frustrated, June sat down one day, swooshed her skirt around her . . . pondered awhile . . . and finally saw her way clear. Why not clasp the handle between her knees, bend the blade over her left leg, and hammer with the mallet in her right hand? As fast as you can say "Art can saw from Arkansas," June was sawing onstage . . . like a lady.

To top it off, Leon's clever sister-in-law also discovered that by placing the tip of her right toe on the floor and jiggling her right knee she could achieve a quivering tremolo in the saw blade that added emotional expression to the music, similar to a pianist's pedal control or a violinist's fingering technique. The vibration extended the tone, enabling June to sustain several notes with one whack of the mallet.

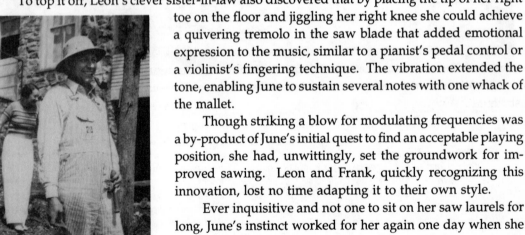

Though striking a blow for modulating frequencies was a by-product of June's initial quest to find an acceptable playing position, she had, unwittingly, set the groundwork for improved sawing. Leon and Frank, quickly recognizing this innovation, lost no time adapting it to their own style.

Ever inquisitive and not one to sit on her saw laurels for long, June's instinct worked for her again one day when she was practicing her single-string violin made from a garden rake. Spying her saw in the corner, June grabbed it and drew her bow across the blunt edge. Well, scratch my back, it hummed! The sweet sound floated smoothly on the air, marred only by the rasp of the bow against the metal. That

Frank "Cicero" Weaver, circa 1937 (woman unknown), Springfield, Missouri (contributed by Ray E. Wilhite, a cousin to the Weavers)

was easily remedied: June rubbed her bow with resin or tar soap just before playing, and rejoiced at the result. Now who was getting the sawpplause? Copycats Frank and Leon soon saw the light, dropped their hammers and never looked back.

The Trio

Billed as the Weaver Brothers 'n' Elviry, the trio was promptly signed by Alex Pantages of the Interstate Vaudeville Circuit. Later they signed with the Radio-Keith-Orpheum (RKO) circuit and toured the United States and Europe. It was during this time that the "true Polynesian," Kale W. Kaleialii (or Charlie, as he is known in the entertainment field), met the Weavers. He remembers them well, due to a little run-in. "I'd been playing the saw professionally since the early 1920s," Charlie writes, "and on vaudeville the Weaver brothers tried to prevent me from performing, claiming they had invented the musical saw!"

Naturally, Kaleialii (from Sunland, California) was indignant. He had learned to play the saw during the winter of 1912 in Baden-Baden, Germany. His teacher, he says, was the trade school master, Gus, who, with his snowy hair and white beard, resembled Kris Kringle as he rapped out "Oh! Tannenbaum" and "Silent Night," using a big spike with a wad of spirit gum on the end.

The Weaver family's possessive attitude about the musical saw is understandable. Trailing from Leon's dusty path in Springfield in 1904 were more than thirty years on stage and screen. The Weaver Brothers 'n' Elviry became one of America's most successful musical acts on the vaudeville circuit, and eventually they followed the "yellow brick road" to the Land of Hollywood, where they appeared in eleven films, including "Swing Your Lady," starring Ronald Reagan, Humphrey Bogart, and Penny (Blondie) Singleton.

Today, at the Ralph Foster Museum, located at Point Lookout, Missouri (and known as the Smithsonian of the Ozarks), you can see mementos of the Weavers' years in show business.

The Weavers' contributions to musical sawing still shape how sawyers approach the instrument. Without them, windstorms and hoot owls might still be just a clever whistling act.

If You Can Sing, Whistle or Hum a Tune

F ollowing the Weavers' seductive sawing act in 1919, Clarence Mussehl left Milwaukee's Majestic Theatre little realizing that his initial attraction to the instrument would evolve into a lifelong project. As luck would have it, the twenty-five-year old Mussehl's father was a building contractor, so of course there were saws lying around just waiting to be stroked. Or, more accurately, Clarence would later tell people, "I pounded, prodded and bowed away

for weeks to no avail. I tried them all and just couldn't get a thing out of them!"

Years later, in 1970, when L.J. Ganshert (Gratiot, Wisconsin) visited Mussehl, the forefather of the professional musical saw told Ganshert that one day he had been so disgusted with his failure to play the saw that he threw it down. BOINNNG! BOINNGGG! rang out, convincing the frustrated Mussehl that the saw did in fact have music in it and there must be a knack to playing it.

Trial and error and perseverance, our saw friends tell us, is the motto for any novice sawyer. No less so for Clarence. Picking up "this devilish instrument," he worked with it until he discovered the secret of bending the blade, which in turn

Clarence Mussehl, founder in 1921 of Mussehl & Westphal, Fort Atkinson, Wisconsin, the first professional musical saw company in the world (contributed by Mary Kay Dawson, owner of Mussehl & Westphal)

produced the ringing tones. "You have to put some pressure on the tip of the blade with your thumb," he told Rob Fixmer of the *Capital Times*, in August 1978, "and pull up with your fingers, forming an S or double curve in the blade."

Clarence's experience with other instruments (like the banjo, piano, harmonica, and ukulele) had helped him to develop a good ear for music, and, gradually, he learned to maneuver the blade to achieve precise tone intervals. Once he had mastered this, he could play almost any tune.

Dance Bands

The man who would end up spending fifty-nine years changing attitudes about the underrated instrument found himself in good company. Between World War I and the Great Depression, the saw was played with ever-growing sophistication by professional musicians. Tremendously popular during the early twentieth century as a solo instrument and as part of musical ensembles performing on the vaudeville stage, the handsaw's reputation was now further enhanced as a romantic interlude for dancers. Many band leaders like Fred Waring, Paul Whiteman, and B.A. Rolfe featured the "silvery sounds of the slithery steel" as a unique musical addition for their dance audience's pleasure. Paul Whiteman, then the acknowledged King of Jazz, engaged Willie Hall, who played the musical saw and the bicycle pump with equal facility. Rolfe (who used to be heard on the Lucky Strike Cigarettes radio program) was an early supporter of Stanley Davis, the saw virtuoso for "Rima's Song" in *Green Mansions*. Like Mussehl, Davis had been inspired to take up the saw after hearing the Weavers in a Brooklyn vaudeville house.

As for Clarence, he had often picked banjo with his brother Art's orchestra. Now he occasionally substituted the saw. The reaction from people who wanted to learn how to play this rippling metal strip was so overwhelming that in 1921 Clarence wrote and published a set of instructions. He sold quite a few copies, too. "But that got me into a lot of trouble," he told Fixmer, "because people didn't have a saw with music in it. The steel wasn't right."

Suddenly, what had been a simple fascination erupted into a passionate mission. Clarence was faced with a real challenge: Find a *musical* saw; one that, like any other perfected instrument, would consistently offer reliable tones.

Clarence stopped selling his instruction book, packed a bag, and began his quest for a proper musical saw.

The Quest

One can only imagine the head-nodding uh-huhs and sideways glances that were exchanged when our knight-in-search-of-a-blade arrived at the Atkins Saw Company in Indianapolis, Indiana, claiming he was trying to transform a carpenter's tool into a musical instrument. But business was business, and if Clarence Mussehl from Fort Atkinson, Wisconsin, had dreamed up a way to market more saws, the Atkins people were not about to discourage him.

Clarence spent the next couple of weeks in Indianapolis experimenting with several types of steel and trying different dimensions of length, width, and thickness for the blade. It was a tedious process, but by the time he had finished and returned home he had developed the first professional musical saw.

From outward appearances, the major difference in the original musical saw was a lack of teeth, like the French *lame sonore*. But more specifically, with respect to performance quality, the intrepid Mussehl had, in fact, achieved a remarkable first.

By using a softer, thinner, and more pliable English steel in the construction of the blade, Mussehl had increased the professional saw's versatility by expanding its one-octave range to more than two octaves. An ordinary carpenter's saw is made of harder metal that yields only seven or eight notes of irregular quality, compared to a professional musical saw, which offers at least sixteen to twenty truer notes. Some instruments ("Supersaw's" modified Sandvik, for example) will produce over three octaves in the hands of a skilled sawyer, no mean feat for a tapered rectangle of flat metal that has nothing —no keys, strings, frets, valves, stops, or other devices —to automatically determine the selection of specific notes. In view of the saw's complex sound production (discussed in Chapter 9), one can more readily appreciate Mussehl's findings and the importance of a good musical ear for tuning in the scale along the saw's S curve.

Critical Cut

The cut of the saw is critical to the quality of vibration it will produce. What Clarence discovered on his own in 1921 is later illustrated in Jacques Keller's study on the *lame sonore*. For economic reasons (but acoustically deplorable, Keller maintains) two handsaws can be punched (cut) from a single strip of steel. Unfortunately, with respect to the axis of the saw blade, this destroys the symmetry of the grain of the metal, thus accounting for the irregular tones and limited range of an off-the-wall carpenter's saw.

By comparison, when musical saws are punched out on a press the axis runs parallel from end to end, without deviating from a straight line edge to edge. This linear symmetry enhances the vibrations of the blade and contributes to the increased range and tonal quality.

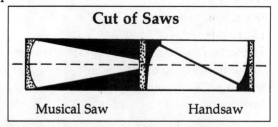

Cut of Saws

Musical Saw   Handsaw

Approximately two inches longer and wider at the heel than regular handsaws, professional musical saws measure from twenty-six inches to thirty-two inches, tip to handle.

Mussehl & Westphal

Within weeks of his visit to Atkins, Clarence had arranged to have saws of English steel manufactured by a Midwest company, and in 1921 he formed Mussehl & Westphal, the first professional musical saw company in the world, which he operated out of his home.

Who is the Westphal in the company name? A mystery, really, whose origins are lost in time much like the beginnings of the musical saw. We know only that Clarence taught a young woman, Marion Westphal, how to play the saw, that they performed as a popular duet during the 1920s, and that eventually Marion drifted away from the act.

Sawing Against the Grain

Contrary to "experts" who said it was not possible to design saws for different tones, Clarence used his knowledge gained at the Atkins company, about steel composition and measurements, to have saws manufactured in four sizes: alto, tenor, baritone, and bass. They proved ideal accompaniment for musical ensembles featuring the piano, Hawaiian guitars, dobros, and harmonicas. The saw's "voices" blended naturally with the simple structures of country music and the light popular tunes of the day.

Cutting a growing reputation among professional entertainers and just-for-fun sawyers, Clarence soon found himself as much a businessman as a musician. "There was so much interest that we used full-page ads in magazines like *Popular Mechanics*, and full-column ads in publications like the *Saturday Evening Post, Collier's*, and *American*, he told the *Capital Times*' Fixmer. "We purchased about fifty ads per month and sold thousands of saws every week."

Clarence Mussehl's slide trumpet-sax, circa 1920s

Clarence Mussehl (from left, with saw) and his musical group The Maestro's Harmonizers, circa 1920s

Jazz-o-nette, 1925

Russian Marr-Hoo-Baw, circa 1920s

Hardware or five-and-dime store saws cost between one and two dollars during this period. Mussehl's musical saws sold for about twice the price; and for another dollar, the sawyer received a lump of resin, a bow and mallet, instructions, and a carrying case.

Needless to say, Mussehl's modified blades trimmed the purists' claim that any old carpenter's saw would sing. Sawyers soon divided over whether a professional musical saw or one destined for the woodpile made a better instrument. The issue —debated as sharply today as in the 1920s —has never been settled.

Even major saw companies became embroiled. E.C. Atkins and the Simonds Saw and Steel Company of Fitchburg, Massachusetts, for example, claimed that any of their stock saws would produce satisfactory music. On the other side of the saw, were Mussehl and the Henry Disston Company (then in Philadelphia; the manufacturing division is now located in Danville, Virginia), both insisting that a true musical saw must be ground to more precise specifications than a carpenter's tool.

In 1938, the Disston Company's hardware sales manager, George Hopf, outlined for the *New Yorker's* Lucille Fletcher, the qualifications of a good musical saw, beginning with the advice that it be a straightback and not a skewback saw, which, due to its curved shape, is incapable of a consecutive scale. Second, the blade must be smooth and not crimped, Hopf maintained, to ensure that the notes will run through the entire blade. Third, a musical saw should be ground flat (which produces the same gauge or thickness at the top and bottom, front to back), rather than taper ground (which is thinner at the front, thus interfering with the purity of the notes). In conclusion, Hopf said, "The gauge of grinding in a musical saw must be a slack 19. If a saw is ground much less than 19 gauge it will be too limber and will produce double tones, which are difficult to control. If ground much heavier than 19, the range of notes that can be produced will be too limited."

Even with the above considerations, however, professional musical saws are not consistent in tone. "There is only one way to tell if a saw is a worthy musical instrument," Hopf told Fletcher, "and that is to play it." At the height of the 1920s' saw craze, late-leaving employees could hear the Disston Company's sales manager in his office, playing cadenzas with a mallet. Noted Fletcher, for every hundred saws Hopf auditioned, he would find seven or eight fine instruments.

More than Sawdust

The controversy about which blade made the best musical instrument added up to more than sawdust for Mussehl & Westphal. Sales reportedly peaked to about 30,000 units per year during the 1920s and 1930s. Clarence had to hire eight full-time employees to fill the orders, and one woman spent the day just slitting open the incoming mail. It was an unprecedented and never-again-matched acceptance of the musical saw as a true instrument, which was used by musicians of every category.

The Depression put a dent in soaring sales, however, and the sweetest music this side of heaven hit a sour note as people scratched for jobs rather than for entertainment. Business dropped to zero in the thirties, Clarence recalled, and then got worse with the advent of the Second World War, causing him to hang up his saw as far as the company was concerned. "There wasn't any steel available for such extravagance as musical saws and I couldn't make a living, so I went to work as a salesman for a specialty paint company."

Latched company doors did not mean silent saws, though, and Clarence continued his one-man crusade by performing as a soloist and lecturer on the musical saw until the mid-1950s, when he decided it was time to unlock Mussehl & Westphal. "But the business never reached the volume of the twenties because of changes in the type of music being played," he lamented. "The saw just isn't adapted to jazz or fast-tempo music."

A Change Saw

Not only had America's taste in music changed, so had Mussehl's product. His mail order package had formerly included a violin bow strung with horsehair. But the price of horsehair had skyrocketed to the point that a bow in the 1950s cost more than the violin it was intended for. Not willing to concede defeat, Clarence substituted synthetic fibers and was pleased to observe, "When the bow's all resined up it sounds just as good as a horsehair one."

Also, in the wake of rising costs and razor-thin sales, he decided to sell only the tenor saw; and he no longer made the elaborate 14-karat gold-plated model (a dollar's worth of gold in 1926), with colored rhinestones studding the mahogony handle. The gold-plated model was once the epitome of musical saw glitz and glamour in the field of entertainment. It cost about $25 in 1937, and today is a priceless possession for a sawyer fortunate enough to own one.

As the fifties turned sixty, then seventy, and the music public swung from rock-around-the-clock strains to those more in keeping with its back-to-nature lifestyle, a nostalgia for ethnic touchstones emerged. Performers like Bob Dylan and the Grateful Dead adapted Nashville sounds to modern instrumentation, consequently breathing new life into the old country and swing rhythms of the 1920s and 1930s.

Fort Atkinson became a mecca of sorts, with Clarence the resident musical Merlin. "When you sing, whistle or hum, your musical ear tells you how to move your lips and tongue to carry the tune," he counseled. "You do it without thinking. And when you play the musical saw, your ear tells you how far to bend the blade for the proper notes. Playing the saw is like singing or whistling —nothing to it."

Those who shared his love for this folk instrument sought him out, exchanged stories, improved their bowing, and always left Clarence's home with the feeling they had stroked saws with a legend.

"I met Clarence around 1975, about three years before he died," writes folk singer Art Thieme, from Peru, Illinois. "I looked him up and purchased one of the last 28-inch saws he had in his basement. He was a great man, one of my 'professors'. That's where folk singers have to go to find the old songs —directly to the older people in the community. Clarence was a real find for me . . . a link to the lumber camp days when the pine woods rang with the sounds of musical saws after work, as entertainment."

Art Thieme was not alone in tracing a path to Clarence's door in 1975. Another man that year also considered Mussehl & Westphal's founder a real discovery. Or maybe it was the other way around, with the eighty-year-old Clarence finding a young airlines pilot, Daniel T. Wallace, practically in his backyard.

Wallace lived in Delavan, twenty-five miles south of Fort Atkinson, and the aura of fate clings to his meeting with Clarence like the chance encounter sixty years earlier between

Mussehl and Leon Weaver. In the same way that the older man did not initially realize that his simple fascination with the saw would evolve into a lifetime of committed promotion, neither did Dan Wallace suspect his future involvement with it when he stumbled across the blade tucked away in his grandmother's attic. But he had a good musical ear, and he could sing, whistle, and hum a tune. . . .

More Than Just an Old Saw

Dan Wallace, Delavan, Wisconsin

The gleaming stones in the saw handle caught Dan Wallace's eyes long before the music reached his ears.

"It was a beautiful thing with a golden blade and a polished wood handle," he said, "which was decorated with inset 'jewels,' and imprinted on the blade were the words, PROFESSIONAL MUSICAL SAW, Mussehl & Westphal, Fort Atkinson, Wisconsin."

The elaborately decorated saw dated from the early 1920s and had belonged to Wallace's grandfather, Robert Parker Davis Claybaugh, who died before Dan was born. Years later, rummaging around in his grandmother's attic, the adolescent boy found the saw and an old horsehair bow and was captivated by the strange possession of a man he had never known.

"Once in awhile I'd get it out and try to play the fool thing," the forty-two-year-old former U.S. Marine recalled in an article that he wrote for the *North Country Folk*, published in March 1981. "But the results were never all that grand and after a bit I'd usually tire of it and back into the closet the old saw would go." Then one day the dark-haired, pipe-smoking first officer for American Airlines unlocked the saw case and opened a hobby that would eventually develop into a business.

"I never thought much about that old saw. It was just one of those fascinating things that kids like to experiment with. It's hard to believe now just how important it has become to me, some thirty-five years later."

After starting up a part-time saw sharpening business, Wallace remembered his grandfather's treasure. Digging it out of the closet in 1971, he discovered the gold-plated saw had lost some of its shine. "But there was still a lot of music left in it and with a little more patience and experience, I was soon able to coax the saw back to life." The task was made easier with a set of instructions he had sent for from Mussehl & Westphal, after reading an ad for the musical saw in *Popular Science* magazine. "In a short time I became quite proficient, and before long I was entertaining friends and relatives with very little encouragement."

Memorable Meeting

As a member of Delavan's Kiwanis Club in 1975, Dan was responsible for getting together a weekly program, and it occurred to him that "the fellows might like to learn a little more about the history and background of this unusual instrument." With that in mind —and little dreaming that the company of Mussehl & Westphal comprised only the octogenarian sawyer— Wallace contacted the Fort Atkinson company to invite someone to speak to the Kiwanis members. He received an enthusiastic, "Sure, I'd be glad to!" from Clarence.

"My life hasn't been the same since," Dan exclaimed. "Clarence was still very active, full of fun, and having a wonderful time entertaining folks with his musical saws. We hit it off right from the start and that evening I had the chance to play along with him, using my grandad's old saw."

It was the beginning of a great friendship, with Mussehl telling the sawyer half his age, "Next to me, you're just about the best saw player I've come across."

That first evening's meeting unrolled into three years of saw talk and perform- ances with the elderly gentleman, as well as helping him to fill orders when the pilot-sawyer was home between flights. These moments were special to Dan, especially one evening in September 1978, when they were returning from a gig in Wausau, Wisconsin. The two men had stopped for a cup of coffee and a bite to eat, and Mussehl confided that it was about time for him to retire from the professional musical saw business. How did he, Dan, feel about being the "heir apparent" to Mussehl & Westphal?

Delight mixed with an overwhelming sense of obligation was how Wallace reacted. "When a person entrusts you with something that has been such a large part of his life for so many years, it is truly an honor. After all, Clarence had sixty years of experience to pass along."

Sixty years versus sixty days. Late in October 1978, just weeks after their conversation —"It was kind of prophetic," mused Wallace —Clarence Mussehl hung up his musical saw for the last time, ending a significant chunk of saw lore by a man who had contributed six decades of his life to developing and marketing musical saws around the world.

'Sawll in the Family

"Since then I've been doing all that I can to keep the musical saw and the memory of Clarence Mussehl alive," Wallace explained. "This little business has allowed my wife and me to play a part in preserving a portion of America's folk history."

The Wallace family (front row, from left): daughters Linda and Joan; Mary Kay Dawson; sons Dan and Jim; (back row, from left): son John and Carl Wallace (Dan's brother)

To GRIT reporter Mickey Cioffi, in May 1981, Wallace emphasized, "My goal is to revitalize the instrument, make more people aware of it, and have some fun with it."

As good as his word, Dan stepped up production, and with a savvy sense of marketing to a reviving interest in folk music, he began selling between 1,500 and 2,000 saws annually, compared to the hundred or so mailed out each year that he had worked with Clarence.

Wallace advertised in a number of magazines, including GRIT, *Mother Earth News*, *Country Journal*, and *Early American Life*, among others. Operating out of his home (another preserved bit of American history; it is over one hundred years old), the musically inclined Wallace family (including brother Carl, Dan's wife, Mary Kay, and their children: Jim, Dan, Joan, Linda, and John) fell under the saw's spell and got involved. John designed the logo that is etched on the blade; Carl fit handles and smoothed the non-serrated edge; Jim, keen on learning everything his father knew about the instrument, became the family's "saw expert"; and everyone helped package the

Mary Kay Dawson and Carl Wallace, with Dan's saw collection

mail orders. The contents had not changed significantly since Mussehl's day, and included a tenor saw with a carrying case, a felt-tipped mallet, a dowel bow and a string bow, four strings, a rosin cake, instructions, and a recording of a sawyer playing harmony to various songs, so the beginning sawyer could play duets.

Said Wallace, "We've been trying to breathe new life into this old folk instrument and I think our efforts are proving worthwhile. Each day the mail brings us letters from folks everywhere. Here's one from Tatsuo Hamano, a marine biologist in Japan; another one from an orthopedic technician in Brooklyn, Moses "Maestro" Josiah, who plays gospel music. Others write to tell us that they have been playing for several years and just want to say hello. Many hadn't seen the saw advertised for quite some time and are glad to find that the company of Mussehl & Westphal is still in business."

Dan Wallace was, of course, his own best advertisement. His job with American Airlines provided him with many opportunities to promote the musical saw around the world. But toting his instrument through airports, cocooned in its rifle-like case, often provoked stares and made security officials nervous. So, like some of our other traveling sawyers who report similar experiences, Dan occasionally had to unzip his case, withdraw the suspicious object and saw away everyone's fears.

Although approached by television promoters who urged him to capitalize on the classic name of Mussehl & Westphal for advertising other products, Wallace spurned such offers, saying, "This is a folksy instrument that doesn't need to be abused. The thing would lose its personality and then it's not fun anymore."

The fun, unfortunately, ended abruptly for Dan Wallace on October 15, 1982, when the two-seat Luscomb airplane that he was piloting crashed in a cornfield near Delavan. Although his experience with the musical saw spanned far fewer years than those of Clarence Mussehl, Dan's dedication was every bit as sincere. "It would be a shame if this truly American art form were allowed to peter out," he said, adding that in 1981 another milestone in the revival of the musical saw had been reached by his brother Tim, who played it in the New York play "Five O'Clock Girl." Exclaimed Dan, "After an absence of fifty-seven years, the musical saw has returned to Broadway!"

Today, under the direction of Mary Kay Dawson, the company of Mussehl & Westphal continues the long-held tradition that the professional musical blade is more than just an old saw.

PART II

CHAPTER FIVE

There's a Song in My Saw

P atience and perseverance are necessary ingredients for any would-be sawyer, but probably no one has been more patient and persevering than CHARLES A. WARREN (Pisgah Forest, North Carolina). Charles waited thirty-nine years before he finally bought his musical saw —truly a deliberated purchase.

"When I was twelve years old, I saw an advertisement for a Mussehl & Westphal musical saw with a violin bow in GRIT, a weekly newspaper that was usually sold by some kid in the community. [Billed as America's Greatest Family Newspaper, GRIT dates from 1882 and is still published at Williamsport, Pennsylvania.] My grandfather was a carpenter and mason, and at times I had heard him play a few notes on his handsaw by bending it into an S-shape and striking it with his thumb. So I thought it would be great to have a saw that could be played with a bow. It cost $12.95. I snipped the ad out, thinking I might order one."

But that was during the Second World War, "and we had what we needed before we had what we wanted," Warren says. The musical saw was "put on the back burner," not to be rekindled until about 1945. By this time sixteen-year-old Charles had learned to play his grandfather's violin —"or fiddle, as most country folks called it then" —and decided he wanted one of his own. By raising pigs and a calf and selling them he was able to buy his first violin, but the notion of a singing saw still intrigued him and he sent off for new literature from Mussehl & Westphal. "By now, of course, the price had gone up to $14.95, so I put the information away and decided to wait awhile longer."

The boy finished school, left home, grew to manhood, and got married. By 1955, Warren says, "The saw just never had high enough priority. I was twenty-six years old and the saw was $27.95, and I thought, maybe someday . . . "

To cut a long story short, in March 1981 Charles finally ordered the oft-suspended musical saw, for $64.70, but he did so with some reservation. "I didn't tell anyone about it because I wanted to see if I could play it first. If not, I planned to put it in my woodworking tools and just say that it was a special saw."

Not to worry, however. By the second or third day, buoyed by the refrains emanating from Jim "Supersaw" Leonard's recording, Charles was sawing his own tunes, adding to an already impressive collection of music-makers that include the violin, accordion, guitar, dulcimer, banjo, mandolin, Cord-A-Rama, and various mouth instruments. "Although my favorite is the violin, the most challenging is the musical saw. I love it and often ask myself why I waited so long to get one. My family loves it too, when I'm NOT playing it!"

Supersaw

It's a bird . . . It's a plane . . . It's SUPERSAW! So reads the English caption emblazoned across the page of an otherwise Japanese newsletter that features *sensei* (teacher) JIM

LEONARD on the cover. Forwarded by marine biologist Tatsuo Hamano, the *Folk Village* newsletter from the Fisheries Department of Kyushu University in Fukuoka carried an article in March 1982 about saw music in the United States. That was *after* Jim had achieved his Master Sawyer status. "Before that, when I first started sawing in 1975," he says, "I chased all the dogs and cats in the neighborhood —and my family, too —into the hills during my first few days of practice."

Since then, Jim, a self-employed gas appliance repairman from Santa Ana, California, has often rosined his bow and performed solo or with an ensemble. He has

Jim "Supersaw" Leonard, 1984
(Allan J. de Lay, photographer)

appeared on radio, at major California theme parks (including Disneyland, Knott's Berry Farm, and Six Flags Magic Mountain), bluegrass festivals, and a number of dining establishments ranging from That Pizza Place in Carlsbad, California, to the Hollywood Hilton.

In 1987, with Frank Holley and Patricia Graham, he appeared on KNBC-TV's "Silver Linings," with host Christopher Nance; on CBS-TV's "The Morning Program," hosted by Mariette Hartley and Rolland Smith; and, with Holley, Graham, and Roland Hill, he performed in a music video with the well-known rock group "Kansas."

His television debut corresponded with the original airing of the "Gong Show" on April 14, 1976. "I got beat out by a cute baton twirler," he says, recalling his rendition of "Spanish Eyes." "Of a possible thirty points, Jamie Farr and Ansel Williams each gave me ten and Phyllis Diller gave me nine. I threatened Phyllis with the saw." The "Gong Show" went off the air for a few years, but was revived in July 1988, and Jim was invited to reappear on the show's first new program.

Obviously, Jim is hooked on the musical saw; six, to be exact, including the last gold-plated saw made by Mussehl & Westphal. He also has two Sandvik "Stradivarius" models; one is a rare baritone saw with a four-octave range, a gift from Toshitaka Onoe, a distributor for Sandvik AB in Japan.

Jim Leonard's musical saws, (from left): Sandvik, stock hardware saw; Mussehl & Westphal, 1980 model, modified; Sandvik Swedish "Stradivarius," modified; Mussehl & Westphal, 1983 model, now made to Jim's specifications; Sandvik "Stradivarius," no modifications; Sears stock carpenter's handsaw (Jim Leonard, photographer)

From the beginning Jim was exhilarated by the challenge of learning to play the instrument as perfectly as possible, without a hint of the nerve-jangling scri-i-i-tch so often heard as bow meets steel. According to Jim, "The noise resembles a cross between stepping on a cat's tail and drawing your fingernail down a blackboard."

"Supersaw" (who does not read notes and improvises on several musical instruments) devoted every spare moment to musical sawing, and finally developed a new method that enabled him to play faster without squeaking his bow. By September 1979, with the first Festival of the Saws in Santa Cruz on the calendar, he felt ready to join the largest known gathering of sawyers in recent history, plus a multitude of curiosity seekers and heavy-metal devotees. In fact, more sawyers arrived for the event than the program could handle and it appeared that Jim would not have an opportunity to play, but the festival coordinator, Margie McMahon, squeezed him onstage at the last minute. The audience's reaction to his performance set musical sawing on its teeth, and established Jim as a skilled sawyer, simply for doing what came naturally to him.

"All the old-timers got up ahead of me and said only slow tunes like ballads and waltzes could be played on the saw. They said it had limitations when it came to playing fast songs. Well, nobody had ever told ME that! I played 'Twelfth Street Rag' and 'Tico Tico' for my two selections and really blew some folks' minds!"

A standing ovation was Jim's reward as he was joined onstage by Moses Josiah and Dan and Jim Wallace to play several more numbers. "Tom Scribner was the master of ceremonies and he called me the 'Supersaw' and the nickname has stuck ever since."

A perfectionist to the nth degree, Jim's first record consisted mostly of lightning-paced songs and was the result of over nine-hundred —yes, 900 —hours of work. Recording in his home studio, he often heard a barking dog or a toilet flushing in the background, or an airplane roaring overhead, so he would grit his teeth and rerecord the song as often as necessary until he had a clean-sounding track.

The recording problem was made more difficult, Jim says, because "no sort of pickup [any device, like a microphone, used for receiving and transmitting sound waves] works with a saw, at least I don't know of any and I've tried everything!"

Jim finally settled on a directional microphone, which he placed underneath the saw near the handle, and aimed towards the ceiling, to eliminate as much as possible the sound of the bow rubbing on the saw's edge. To further cut noise, he also used a white horsehair bow, which is a bit finer, and therefore quieter, than a black horsehair bow.

Of his choice of songs, Jim explains, "I tried to get away from the traditional saw playing on my first album. I wanted to give the saw a new dimension, so I recorded fast-scratchin' songs like 'Tico Tico,' 'Beer Barrel Polka,' 'Alexander's Rag Time Band,' 'Under the Double Eagle,' and 'The Robert E. Lee.' I also believe mine is the first attempt to do a multi-saw record."

The album, titled "Super Saw," has been accepted by Washington D.C.'s Smithsonian Institution and the Library of Congress archives, a gesture that Jim considers an honor, but which cannot compare with another form of recognition that strikes a bit closer to home. You will recall that Clarence Mussehl had stopped making the gold-plated saw years ago. But exceptions are the stuff of legends. In 1980, following the release of Jim's record, Dan Wallace (who by this time had taken over Mussehl & Westphal) flew out to California to deliver a saw ordered by Jim and modified to his specifications. Dan, however, had his own "specifications" in mind, and instead of delivering the expected plain steel saw, he presented Jim with a gold-plated instrument inscribed to the Master Sawyer. Said Wallace, "Finally, someone plays the saw without all the other scratchy noises being heard too."

Unearthly Noise

"When a massed bank of possibly a hundred or more saws cuts loose, God Almighty, the pigs will quit littering, coyotes will quit whelping, and the timber wolves will head for the tall uncut! . . . The noise may not be heavenly, but it certainly will be UNEARTHLY!!!"

That's THOMAS JEFFERSON SCRIBNER, a self-proclaimed "olde tyme saw freak," quoted at the 1980 Festival of the Saws, Santa Cruz, California. With his trademark Charlie Chaplin bowler, red socks and matching red suspenders, the chain-smoking Scribner was a plain-spoken man with a colorful background. Born in May 1899, in Duluth, Minnesota, he learned to play the saw a few years after hearing it in a vaudeville show when he was ten years old. Said Scribner, "All the big bands had a saw player in those days —Paul Whiteman, Clyde Doer, Art Hickman —and so did the circus and vaudeville bands."

Tom Scribner, 1980 (Victoria Bolam, photographer)

Who taught him to play?

"Nobody taught me," he told Dan Wallace. "It was just trial and error. It took a year or so before I could get anything out of it. The devil is hard to play. It's been called the hardest instrument in the world. But then a lot of musicians will snort that it's not an instrument at all."

Instrument or not, Scribner turned from his violin to the saw and learned to play so well that vaudeville beckoned. At the ripe old age of sixteen he hit the road to the big time: Duluth, Minneapolis-St. Paul, Chicago, Toledo, Buffalo. Three months later —not older but wiser — he quit, admitting, "I was just too young for anything as heavy as that. All those cancan girls were swarming all over me. It was the saw that turned them on. It finally got to be too much for me."

Finding trees less emotional, he put his saw to use as a lumberjack and spent the next fifty years in the logging camps of Minnesota, Washington, Oregon, and California, courting excitement of a different sort as he made dangerous river runs, from which fifteen percent of the loggers never returned. Noting the stumpy middle finger on his left hand, one realizes there were also other dangers. An accident in 1950, for example, precluded Scribner's violin playing, and almost ended the crusty lumberjack as well. "I fell into a saw mill. I had the choice of taking it head first or with my hand. Ah, decisions," he sighed, "all the time decisions."

Dusting off his musical saw when he was seventy-five, the peripatetic Scribner hit the road again, this time playing to nostalgia-hungry college audiences during the 1970s, who, he said, "were every bit as enthusiastic as those audiences of old. I don't see no difference between 'em." And the girls still loved him, only this time he could handle them better. "Now they come up and kiss me on the cheek and I tell 'em I'll never wash my cheek again," he grinned. "Life is a lot of fun."

The sculpture of Tom Scribner in Scope Park, Santa Cruz, California, 1983 (KUSP photo file; Allan J. de Lay, photographer)

Tom played for years with The Lost Sound ("We were going to call it The Santa Cruz Cut-Ups"), which featured Arlene Sutton on the piano and accordion, and Herman Olson playing "second saw," Tom teased, because it was 1920, a decade after Scribner started musical sawing, before Olson picked up a bow.

Any advice for beginning sawyers?

"Yup, you have to be careful to play opposite the teeth. Otherwise you'll cut your bow to hell."

Art Thieme remembers meeting Tom just before 1983, when Scribner, a lifelong Wobbly, attended an Industrial Workers of the World convention in Chicago. According to Art, the former lumberjack had been dealing with Clarence Mussehl for fifty years by mail, but had never met him. "When Tom told me where he got his saw, his face clouded over and he reverently said 'Fort Atkinson, Wisconsin,' like he was saying 'Mecca.' Mr. Mussehl and 'Fort,' as the natives call it, had taken on a mythical aspect for him."

Tom Scribner inspired his own myth as he traveled the country appearing on television and at county fairs and rodeos, garnering numerous awards and amusing audiences with his laconic sense of humor. He jammed with the likes of Neil Young, George Harrison, Leon Russell, and Larry Hosford. In June 1981, at age eighty-two, he opened a Willie Nelson show. He also performed with rock musicians Country Joe McDonald and Muddy Waters, and really hit it big when he was featured on Johnny Carson's "Tonight Show," and CBS television's "On the Road." "I just wrote to Mr. [Charles] Kuralt. I thought he might want to talk to me," Scribner said.

Bidding farewell to a legend is difficult. Tom's death on September 25, 1982 (a month before the loss of Dan Wallace) prompted Tom Scribner Day in Santa Cruz, where hundreds gathered to pay homage to their folk hero and fellow sawyer, one who thoroughly practiced his own dictum to "yank the musical saw out of the dustbin of history."

Lasting appreciation of this unusual and well-loved character had been marked much earlier, however, with a life-size bronze sculpture depicting Tom as most would remember him: seated along Pacific Garden Mall with his right leg crossed over his left, head cocked and shoulders hunched in concentration above his saw. The work was created by Margie McMahon and dedicated at Santa Cruz's Scope Park in November 1978, as a prelude to the first Festival of the Saws. Tom's sense of humor after the dedication was typical. He had business cards printed identifying him as a saw player, revolutionary, lumberjack emeritus, writer, publisher, editor, veteran, union organizer, columnist, sex symbol, and statue.

Tom Scribner, Santa Cruz Saw Festival; note the microphone under the saw for better pickup, 1982 (Allan J. de Lay, photographer)

(From left) Tom Scribner and Allan J. de Lay, sawyer and official saw festival photographer, from Portland, Oregon, 1982

DAVID WEISS is a musical anomaly. The thin bespectacled man in the black satin-lapeled tuxedo gives the appearance of a principal oboist, which he is, with the Los Angeles Philharmonic; and his bearded visage also resembles that of an Appalachian musician, which, figuratively, he is also. David saws.

"I became interested in the saw in 1981 when I heard one played at a friend's house. I picked it up and was able to play a few notes and promised myself that I would buy one. Shortly thereafter, while the Philharmonic was on tour in Memphis and Nashville —where I thought sure I could buy a 'musical' saw —I shopped around for one, but couldn't find anything but regular hardware store saws." Finally, at the biggest hardware outlet in Memphis, Weiss says, "I settled on a Stanley Handyman, which I still use almost exclusively." He calls it his C-saw because the lowest note in the two-octave range is a concert C.

(From left) Tom Scribner and David Weiss

David carries his seven-dollar Stanley in a banged up violin case, and the only alteration he has made is to coat the handle with silicon glue to prevent it from slipping between his knees. He shuns professional musical saws in general, saying, "If you're going to play a folk instrument, you should play the original." (In all fairness, he adds that for some musical applications he bows a Mussehl & Westphal or a Sandvik "Stradivarius.")

One of the few sawyers to promote this ethereal sounding instrument in orchestral surroundings, David has sawed with the Humboldt State Symphony Orchestra, the Topanga Philharmonic, and the Los Angeles Philharmonic. In July 1985, he was the featured saw soloist when the Los Angeles Philharmonic introduced the instrument for the first time at the Hollywood Bowl, to an audience of more than 17,000. Bowl-goers responded enthusiastically to a medley of American music written for the saw and orchestra by Gary Mandell, who also arranged and produced Weiss's "Saw Virtuoso" album. But, as of yore, David complains, "Some people still cannot believe their ears. They think I'm whistling."

Although trained from an early age to read music (he was studying the piano at age three, the oboe at eleven), Weiss plays the saw by ear. "The greatest difficulty," he says, "is landing securely on pitch when playing fast-paced songs." Nevertheless, he has managed to land on pitch well enough to be a Santa Cruz Saw Festival winner two straight years, and to capture appearances on Johnny Carson's "Tonight Show" and National Public Radio's "All Things Considered," bowing everything from the Beatles and Simon and Garfunkel tunes to Gershwin, Ravel, Satie, Saint-Saens, and Bach.

Weiss even scratched a little *bel canto* while on tour in Italy with the Los Angeles Philharmonic. To do so cost him 6,000 lire, endless paperwork, and four tiresome trips to two government offices. BUT he got an official permit to play his saw on the streets of Florence —well, one street, anyway, for a few minutes. Street musicians are rare in Italy (due to the permit procedure, perhaps?) and soon a hundred people had knotted around this curiosity. More joined the clutch until pedestrian traffic stood still at high noon in the Piazza Signoria. A dour policeman broke through, demanded to see the *signor* musician's permit, and promptly put a kink in David's blade. See a saw, yes. Saw a C, no. While the policeman untied traffic, David set off to find a more hospitable piazza before his precious permit expired at one o'clock.

Commenting that "heavy-metal music is something you can sink your teeth into," Weiss adds that his pursuit of an unorthodox instrument is perfectly in character: "Oboists are known as oddballs." But he dismisses any notion that he will eventually switch to the electric saw, explaining, "That would really be a shock."

David Weiss, sawyer and principal oboist with the Los Angeles Philharmonic

Them Bones, Them Bones . . .

Dr. VERNON "Sawbones" REMELIN, formerly a chiropractor from Bell, California, took up the saw at the ripe old age of ten after seeing a sawyer at a Christmas party. Playing "Santa," Vern's father ordered one of Mussehl & Westphal's gold-plated saws with the bejeweled handle, which Vern (known then as "The Boy Saw Player") used for many years in the Upper Mississippi Valley of Illinois. Initially, his mother accompanied him on the piano, and he earned the princely sum of two dollars a day, which increased to five dollars as he grew older and more experienced.

"I left Moline in 1937 and settled in Southern California," he said, "and I didn't play very often because I didn't have anyone to accompany me." As the years rolled by, however, Vern noted that he "became more interested in sawing when country western music came into the picture." In what spare time he could manage, he accepted invitations to perform with country western groups, as well as the Southeast Dixieland Jazz Ensemble, until January 1985, when Vern joined some of our other sawyers at the Great Saw-Off finale.

The Stand-up

Saw fans look up to MORGAN J. COWIN. He is T-A-double L. So tall, in fact, that he plays his saw standing up, partly because that is the stance he observed with his first sawyer in Copenhagen, Denmark. But a more compelling reason, Morgan grins, "is because I'm thin and don't have enough padding on my rear to sit around very long. Also, I've found that I can make faster changes in pitch while standing."

The San Francisco photographer sent for his musical saw in 1971, after glimpsing a Mussehl & Westphal ad in the *Whole Earth Catalog*. "At the time, I was a music minor at Idaho State University in Pocatello, with classic guitar as my main instrument." But in those days, Morgan points out, "*Everyone* was playing guitar, and my saw always received better reactions from people."

A photo assignment to East Africa during the mid-seventies dulled his saw playing for awhile because he took along only his guitar. But after his return to the United States in 1976, Cowin says, "I sawed off and on until 1980, when I really got serious about it and began sharpening my skills."

Now the guitar collects dust and the saw gathers awards, like first place at the 1982 Festival of the Saws in Santa Cruz. Cowin (who plays classical music as well as country, folk, and popular) was asked in 1983 to play at the US Festival in San Bernardino. "What a production!" he exclaims, adding that his wife Lori, a singer, Michael Wanger, a guitarist he met in East Africa, and Bill Heier, a two-man ripsawyer, joined him onstage. The group performed at the US Festival the same day as Willie Nelson, Emmy Lou Harris, Waylon Jennings, Hank Williams, Jr., and Riders in the Sky. "We had a great time playing and singing with the other talents well into the night," Cowin recalls.

(From left) Morgan Cowin, Michael Wanger, Bill Heier, September 1983, Festival of the Saws, Santa Cruz, California (Allan J. de Lay, photographer)

A Tall Saw

Saucer-size eyes are always riveted on BILL HEIER's 5' 8" two-man rusty ripsaw. Immense jagged teeth. No handles. Jokes Bill, "They better pay attention, 'cause if I slip someone in the crowd might lose his head."

Born in Igloo, South Dakota, and now calling San Francisco home, Bill found his ripsaw in a farmer's abandoned woodshed in Chico, California. While experimenting with various sound effects in 1973 for electronic music and movie soundtracks, Bill says, "I discovered I could pound out an understandable melody line on the saw with a tympani mallet."

Invited in 1980 to compete at the Santa Cruz Festival of the Saws, Bill decided he "wasn't quite ready to do that," so he told the festival officials that he had lost his saw. "But actually I hid it." The next year, however, Bill gave in and made his sawing debut as one-third of KUSP Radio's Listener-Sponsored Trio, which featured Heier and Victoria Bolam on saws and John "Champagne Charlie" Hoffman on guitar. The trio brought the house down with a Stephen Foster medley and rousing renditions of "Ghost Riders in the Sky" and "Rawhide."

What about the sawing competition?

"The judges laughed so hard at my ripsaw and enjoyed it so much that they created a special category and awarded me first prize."

Since then, Heier has chalked up credits at various clubs and events, including San Francisco's Plough Shares and the Fremont Hotel's Venetian Room, the Freight and Salvage in Berkeley, and the 1983 US Festival held in San Bernardino.

(From left) Morgan J. Cowin and Bill Heier (KUSP photo file)

Saw Wit

A wild and witty testament on how to create miracle ads seems the least likely place to find information on the musical saw. Unless, of course, you happen to be the multi-talented San Francisco advertising consultant ROBERT C. PRITIKIN, publicist extraordinaire, author of *Christ Was an Ad Man*, and America's self-acclaimed foremost sawist. "It's a billing I immodestly gave myself, but who would dare to challenge it?" Pritikin remarks candidly on page 101 of his book.

Who indeed? Because between the pages of public relations prose and racy ad writing for wine, women, and song, Robert has included a section on how he publicized his album, "There's a Song in My Saw," that does as much for boosting the musical saw as . . . well, as Christ did for promoting Christianity. "Certainly America's Foremost Concert Sawist would pull out all the PR plugs in promoting his own album," he writes.

A sawist for over twenty-five years, Pritikin declares, "My relief from the incessant pressure of creating advertising ideas has been to create music. At first I performed only for my quiet pleasure and psychotherapeutic needs. The instrument of my choice was an ordinary carpenter's saw."

Eventually, he achieved "a modicum of proficiency," leading to guest appearances on radio, television, and concert stage, including a performance in 1983 with the Los Angeles Philharmonic, where, he says, "The guest conductor, Leonard Bernstein, was kind enough to sign my saw."

The production of Robert's record album was the result of an appearance on a San Francisco television show. Formally outfitted in white tie and tails, French-cuffed shirt, and spit-shine shoes, he claims, "I performed 'Moonlight Sawnata' with a full baroque orchestral accompaniment, and was approached by record promoters who felt an album featuring my curious talent might have some commercial potential."

Robert C. Pritikin

The copywriting for the album jacket (oversawn by Robert and deliberately silly to attract the attention of radio disc jockeys) advertised the record as "bringing to the popular classics a musical, magical sawsory that cuts through all tradition. . . . The melancholy wail of the saw reaches octaves almost inaudible to the human ear. You may be well advised to lock your dog in the garage. . . . It is regrettable that this, [Pritikin's] finest album, is his last, because when he cut this album, he inadvertently cut off his left leg."

Those were marvelous madcap days, Pritikin reveals, but the big question is, How well were his albums selling? Initially, not well at all. A spot ad in *Playboy* magazine, however, caused his phone to jangle off the hook, and Pritikin says he was able "to divest myself of thousands of my distressed albums," which he had stored in the garage of his genuine Playboy Pad (the subject of an article in the magazine's June 1973 issue). Requests from disc jockeys and talk-show hosts followed, generating even more publicity and sales, which delighted Pritikin.

Even more important, we think, the activity created much-needed visibility for the lost art of musical sawing in general, and that is really sawmething else.

Through the Years

S.A.W. spells Shirley A. Wigginton, called "Wig" by his friends, PHIL HALL recalls. "He was an expert saw player. I met him during the deep depression of the thirties. Neither of us was working at the time and Wig, who had a refrigerated truck, suggested we sell fish between San Diego and Phoenix, Arizona. While en route we stopped overnight in Yuma. Taking a walk to stretch my legs, I went into a radio station and told them about Wig's saw playing, and they asked me to bring him around for a tryout. Upon hearing him, they asked Wig to play once a week on the radio for half an hour. I learned through friends in Yuma that he was a great hit. Because of this I took an interest in saw playing and Wig passed his knowledge on to me. Originally, I played a Disston finish saw, but later I changed to a Mussehl & Westphal saw that I bought in Fort Atkinson. It has a longer range and is more flexible."

Phil, a resident of Alpine, California, carried his saw with him during the Second World War and "played in the barracks, on the destroyer, in the Canal Zone, on the East Coast, at Casablanca [Morocco, Northwest Africa], and at Londonderry [Northern Ireland]."

With the end of the war and his return to civilian life, Phil worked up several musical groups and played for hospitals, home parties, senior events, radio, and television; something he still does with The Melodeers, who offer "music with a lilt."

WILLIAM C. GOODMAN's first saw "was purchased by my father in March or April 1925, from the G.C. Murphy Five & Dime. I played it with the rubber part of an old pen holder."

Later that year, Goodman tells us, he received "a 14K gold-plated, jewel-studded saw from Mussehl & Westphal for my fifteenth birthday. I gave up playing the piano for my new saw, a special alto that covers three octaves."

Sixty years later, Goodman (Melbourne, Florida) is still gliding a bow across his gold saw. Since his radio debut in 1928, on station WAAT in Jersey City, New Jersey, William has added numerous radio performances on stations in Connecticut, Massachusetts, Michigan, and Toronto, Canada. He has also played for square-dancing and senior citizen clubs in New York and Florida. "My first large audience was 2,000 people at Memorial Hall in Columbus, Ohio, with a 51-piece backup orchestra."

BARNEY LE DUC, who is "seventy-seven years young" by his own accounting in 1986, tells us that he was "reluctantly" given his first saw lesson in 1927, "just before [Charles] Lindbergh flew the ocean. As a high school trombone player in Milwaukie, Oregon, I heard this strange sound from a big-band orchestra on KGW radio. I asked our school orchestra conductor about it, and she said, 'That's my friend. He plays saw.' Later she arranged my first saw lesson with him, and encouraged my saw playing by letting me play with the school orchestra, alternating with the trombone."

Barney continues, "I started out on Dad's old 26-inch Atkins saw —sure a contrast to my teacher's fancy gold-plated, jeweled M & W! Later, I played a Disston D23, and finally purchased a 28-inch tenor saw from M & W, which is really great in tone and takes less effort to play than the others. I've got a 30-inch Charlie Blacklock Special, too, which I like for its deeper tone (F below middle C)."

Like some of our other sawyers, Barney has devised a finger saver: "I split a 2-inch piece of welding hose, then slip it over the tip and tape it on. Sure saves the fingers as they hook over the end of the saw!"

Blacklock Special

Charlie's Band has been playing around the San Francisco Bay area for years, led by CHARLIE BLACKLOCK, who is heard frequently on radio and television stations in that area. He is also the singing saw on a recording of the operetta *The Saga of Pecos Bill on the Eve of Killing His Wife*. "I'm into saw playing all the time," says Blacklock, who, when he saws solo, plays the harmonica simultaneously because the two instruments blend well together.

Charlie distributes his own line of custom manufactured musical saws, the C. Blacklock Special, in four lengths: 26-inch and 28-inch tenor saws; a 30-inch baritone; and a 36-inch special order mini-bass saw.

"At one time I published a booklet on how to play the handsaw. Oak Publications bought the rights from me to include the material in a book titled *How to Play Nearly Everything*, by Dallas Cline" [copyright 1977].

Barney LeDuc

Charlie Blacklock, 1981 (Richard Storck, photographer)

Gospel Truth

M ellifluous and divine is the music he can draw
O ut of the bowels of an ordinary saw
S etting weary hearts at rest
E asing souls which are possessed
S uch genius as this deserves the greatest award

J oyfully he plods along life's weary ways
O bscuring the shadows with the music he plays
S howering pleasures and messages of Christianity
I nspiring those around him by his pure integrity
A spirations as noble as his, which all men applaud
H eaven's blessings and help will have their reward

MOSES E. JOSIAH crowned his early career in musical sawing by playing for the Queen of England during her visit to Guyana in 1964. A native of this former British protectorate [Guyana lies off the northeast coast of South America], Josiah began playing the musical saw in 1947, "after I read in an American magazine about a man making music on a regular cutting saw." As Moses tells it, "My parents cringed from the racket until my mother began to appreciate the haunting melodious notes and ordered that I be left alone."

After experimenting with different blades that he purchased from the hardware store, the "Maestro," as he is known professionally, finally ordered a Sandvik "Stradivarius," and later a saw from Mussehl & Westphal. His musical preference is gospel and classical, for which he has won many awards, the most memorable, he remarks, "being first prize at the 1967 Guyana Music Festival, where I was given a standing ovation."

Through the years, Moses has performed in the Caribbean Islands, the Netherlands Antilles, and the United States. During a visit to New York in 1961, he performed on Ted Mack's "The Original Amateur Hour" and

Moses Josiah, 1987 International Musical Saw Festival and Saw-Off, Northridge, California (Jim Leonard, photographer)

won the talent contest. Soon after, he was invited back for a repeat performance, but, unfortunately, he had already left the United States to return to Guyana.

Moses is no stranger, though, to U.S. musical saw events. Now an orthopedic technician living in Brooklyn, New York, he performs regularly on the East Coast, and has journeyed westward to appear at the Santa Cruz Saw Festival; the Early American Festival in Portland, Oregon; and the International Musical Saw Festival and Saw-Off at Northridge, California.

"I needed another musical instrument about February 1926," says TOBE HEATON, hence his interest in the woodcutter's tool. Tobe cannot remember where he saw his first sawyer, "but it was probably Clarence Mussehl in 1928." On his $2.50 handsaw, Tobe uses a $600 violin bow, which should make heavenly music wherever he goes!

Steve Porter, 1987 International Musical Saw Festival and Saw-Off, Northridge, California (Jim Leonard, photographer)

STEVE PORTER, a videographer-artist in his late thirties, from Ferndale, California, learned to play the saw in 1983, after seeing an ex-logger play at an Old-Timers' Festival in Orick, California. The following year, Steve started walking away with awards at various saw festivals on the West Coast: Best Jazz Saw, Santa Cruz, California, 1984; Best Classical Saw, Portland, Oregon, 1985; Best Classical Saw and Grand Prize, Portland, 1986; Pop-Jazz, First Place, International Musical Saw Festival and Saw-Off, Northridge, California, 1987.

To get the optimum range from his saws, Steve says he modifies them "by cutting or tapering the saw blade down to almost a point at the tip. This increases its range to about two and a half octaves."

Steve has also developed a bowing technique that he calls blocking, "in which I stop the note with the palm of the hand every time I make a new pass or direction with the bow. This stops the sound and keeps the notes from all running together. Blocking is very difficult to do, but it's very effective in making the saw sound like a musical instrument."

From several continents away, FRANCIS R. KASENDA (Limbe, Malawi, Africa), writes that on March 13, 1984 thieves broke into his home while he was sleeping and stole a number of items. They were about to run off with his saw when he awoke and managed to stop them. "It would have been a great, great loss for me," writes Kasenda, who had only recently resumed playing after replacing (with much difficulty) the bow strings, which a friend had broken several years earlier.

Though he was able to save his saw, Kasenda's only saw tape was stolen (one of Clarence Mussehl playing), which effectively severed his only exposure to another sawyer. Originally, in 1977, Kasenda says, "The saw was a very strange thing to me when my father brought it home from the United States. As far as I know, I'm the only sawyer in the country now. There was another at one time, a missionary by the name of Pastor Johnson. I knew him, but I never had the chance to hear him play the saw before he left the country."

Kasenda is a mechanical engineering technician with the Grain and Milling Company in Limbe, and his "greatest wish," he says, in his letter to Jim Leonard, "is to be able to meet other sawyers like you and the rest at a musical saw festival, or even privately, just to share experiences. It is nice to hear news from across the miles —thousands and thousands —about the saw. I'm like one separated from all friends, who, when he receives a note from one, each word contained therein becomes very important."

Clark Niederjohn

Joe R. Hunter (contributed by Larry E. Hunter)

Gary Froiland, 1983

Festival of the Saws, Santa Cruz, 1983 (Allan J. de Lay, photographer)

More Songs in My Saw

How do you play a saw? "Carefully," laughs RAMBLIN' RAY RICKETTS of Fayetteville, Arkansas. A raconteur of tall tales while sawing bluegrass, gospel, and country western for audiences, Ramblin' Ray enlivens his act with accounts of how to achieve vibrato ("by wiggling your fingers like a belly dancer") and how the musical saw originated, a story that Ricketts attributes to his late friend and saw partner Bert Campbell of Lead Hill, Arkansas.

The origin of the musical saw (so goes the tale) is the legend of John Schmidt, a Pennsylvania Dutch lumberjack who fell asleep under a big pine tree. He dreamt that his trusty saw stood up between his knees, grinned, and said, "John, you've treated me pretty well all these years. You keep me sharp, and you don't leave me out in the rain to rust. But you know, John, there's one thing that really bothers me. My back itches somethin' awful! And if you'll just scratch it for me I'll hum some of the most beautiful music you've ever heard this side of heaven."

Well, John felt a little foolish and he looked around to make sure no one was watching, then he reached over and scratched his saw's back with the edge of his finger. Nothing happened. But John was a superstitious fellow who believed that dreams had meaning, so when he woke up and headed for home he pondered the dream all the way and couldn't make any sense of it. A little fiddle scratchin' will soothe me, he thought. Fiddle scratchin'? Saw, scratch . . . fiddle and bow . . . faster than a ripsaw through a gum tree John buzzed up the path, threw open his cabin door, grabbed his fiddle bow off the mantle and drew it across the back of his saw. It hummmmmed heavenly!

Ramblin' Ray Ricketts

Since 1963, Ramblin' Ray has followed that scratch-my-back advice himself. He learned to play on his father's Disston blade, he says, "using the dowel part of a wooden coat hanger as a bow. I played my first saw solo about one week later."

In 1975, Ricketts became a charter member of the Mountain Folks Music Festival at Silver Dollar City, near Branson, Missouri. He holds fifth place in the 1980 Iowa State Music Championships, and in 1982 he sawed his way to first place at the Illinois State Music Competition. Now he plays professionally with the Ozark Mountain Music, a live stage show in Rogers, Arkansas. Says Ramblin' Ray, "It's designed for lotsa pickin' and grinnin' and good clean Ozark entertainment at its best!"

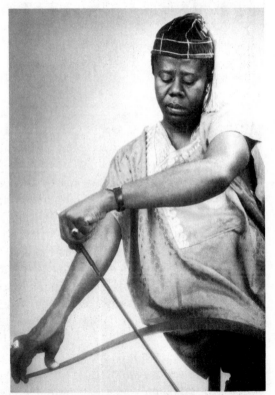

McKinley A. DeShield, Jr.

Diversified Doc

Dressed in native African garb, "Diversified Doc" cuts an imposing figure on the front of his brochure. McKINLEY A. DeSHIELD, JR., lists scientist, philosopher, educator, administrator, athlete, musician, humanitarian, and Christian beneath his photo. Add musical sawyer to that roster.

Place of origin: Monrovia, Liberia, West Africa. Current residence: Greensboro, North Carolina, where "Doc" is a professor of agronomy and a "popularizer," he says, of the musical saw. DeShield's father played the saw in West Africa during the early twentieth century, and so did his brother, Leonard, both an inspiration for his own interest in the instrument, DeShield claims. He started playing in 1959, but did not get serious about musical sawing until 1963, when he was at Nottingham University, England. He has since produced two albums: "He Saws Notes" and "He Cuts and Nails Notes," on which he plays a variety of music, but sacred hymns are the most appealing to him.

Addressing the musical saw's unknown beginnings, DeShield says, "With all respect to

Sam Brignoni

Henry Cassaly

what has been written about its origins, I believe the carpenter's saw, as a musical instrument, may have been brought to the U.S. from Africa, perhaps through captivity [of African slaves]. Most of the naturally-born Africans have used the carpenter's saw since ancient times, and still use it today to generate music, by scraping it very hard, especially during the appearance of Santa Claus and for dancing on ceremonious occasions."

The Show Must Go On

The year was 1948 and an American Armed Forces radio show featuring actress Marlene Dietrich playing the musical saw was scheduled for broadcast. Her saw, however, had been lost in transit. In true the-show-must-go-on fashion, studio officials began scurrying to find a saw, not an easy short-notice task. A now-forgotten musical director remembered that VIC VENT was an accomplished musical saw player. Fortunately, Vic was free when someone called, and, with saw in hand, he quickly arrived on the scene to save the day, thus earning Miss Dietrich's gratitude. She invited him to visit her on the film set of "Foreign Affair," where he obliged the cast and crew with a command performance on the musical saw.

Vic's sawing covers more than sixty-five years, he writes, "beginning in 1920 when I was a ten-year-old boy practicing the mandolin and violin in the rear of my father's Pico Street [Los Angeles] barber shop. At the time, I was being booked by the Walter Trask agency for weekend amateur shows in the neighborhood theaters, and I was consistently winning second or third prizes. Joe Abramson, a representative for the Atkins Saw Company, was one

Vic Vent and Marlene Dietrich, December 1948 (contributed by Vic Vent and reprinted with permission from J.R. Richards, owner, Pasadena Athletic Club, California)

of my dad's customers and he taught me how to play the saw. Within three weeks I had added it to my act, thereby raising my chances of winning to first-prize caliber."

Sharing all these years with his charming wife, Katy, who says, "I don't know one note from another," Vic has logged a lot of saw hours on radio and television: Kate Smith's TV show for CBS in New York, and Los Angeles's CBS Rudy Vallee radio suspense dramas; and he has produced sound effects for cartoons and films, including "Curtain Call at Cactus Creek" (1950) with Donald O'Connor, and "Hi Barbaree." In a telephone conversation from their home in Mesa, Arizona, Katy said, "In 'Hi Barbaree' Vic's saw portrayed a weird G note that was heard by actor Van Johnson every time he was frightened by something."

Vic's saw also horsed around in "My Brother Talks to Horses" (1946), and he provided the celestial sound for the voices in "Black Gold" (1963). In 1966, Vic says, "I spent three days with a fifty-piece orchestra recording the sound track for Warner's 'A Fine Madness,' which starred Sean Connery and Joanne Woodward. John Addison made a separate sixteen-page score for the saw, and I received a beautiful letter complimenting me on my performance."

Vic Vent is still drawing a bow and sawpplause with his group The Music Maestro's, at the Ashford Room, Golden Hills Golf Resort, in Mesa, Arizona.

The Sawduster

Moving eastward from the West Coast, we come to the "Sawduster," RENÉ BOGART of Barre, Massachusetts, who is in his late-late 80s and still sawing away. "I have just TOOO many bookings to quit," says the cousin of the late film actor, Humphrey Bogart.

Trained as a classical cellist, René "started experimenting with miscellaneous saws from the cellar more than fifty years ago." He gradually worked his way up from small-time volunteer engagements to invitations at such prestigious concert establishments as New York's

Emil Richards with tuned circular saw blades

David B. Moore

Allen Givens

Chuck Larkin, sawyer and folk storyteller, Atlanta Arts Festival, 1981

Town Hall and Carnegie Hall. He was the first saw-yer to be invited to play at both auditoriums, and when asked how he got there, re-plied, "PRACTICE!"

As accompaniment, Bogart writes that he prefers "a Steinway Grand Piano, NOTHING ELSE, because many of the electronic means and amplification and so forth detract from the saw's pure tonal qualities."

Although for theatrical effect he sometimes uses a cane or a coat hanger in place of a bow, René stresses, "I NEVER HAMMER A MUSI-CAL INSTRUMENT —GOD FORBID! I don't need nov-elty!"

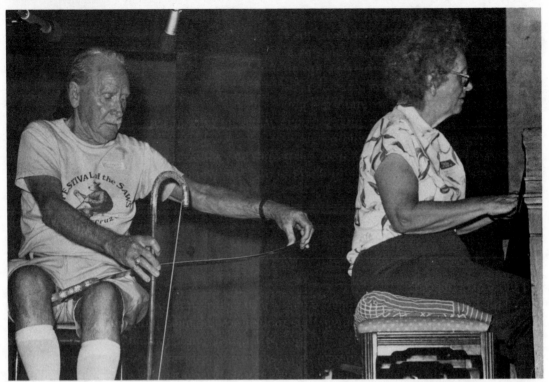

René Bogart sawing with a cane (accompanist unknown), Festival of the Saws, September 1983, Santa Cruz, California (Allan J. de Lay, photographer)

René's credits stretch the length of his saw and include some very successful fund-raising events for the American Cancer Society in Boston, and the Y.M.C.A. Minstrel Shows in Athol, Massachusetts. He has been present at several Santa Cruz saw festivals, and can add the "PM Magazine Show" and NBC-TV's "Today Show" to his performance list.

Bogart is fond of stories and loves to relate how a high school janitor provided him with "one of the more unsettling experiences I've had with my musical saw. A number of years ago, just minutes before I was to perform with the Les Jardienne Trio in a school auditorium, I dashed off to answer Nature's call, leaving my saw lying on a table. When I returned, it was gone! Panicked, I looked around and spotted the janitor ambling away with my saw. 'Hey!' I yelled, and retrieved my instrument just before the curtain went up" . . . leaving a puzzled custodian standing in the wings, no doubt.

René Bogart with John Tuck, master of ceremonies, Santa Cruz Saw Festival, 1983 (Allan J. de Lay, photographer)

Coming to Grips

ART THIEME, the poster says, "Grips the Mind, Binds the Heart." He is a folk singer, multi-instrument musician, raconteur, saw player, and "godawful punster," according to one review, but it is said fondly, and followed with the statement that "when he delivers a song, old or new, serious or silly, you just know, somehow, that it's true. Now, that's an art —and that's Art."

Considered "just plain folk" by many, Thieme is a Chicago native who performs frequently for school programs, at coffee houses and cabarets, and other places of entertainment in the counties surrounding the Windy City. You might even run into this burly fellow during a performance along the East Coast. Says Thieme, "Actually, it's a pretty sparse living sometimes, but my wife and son seem willing to go along with it, and I'm doing what I enjoy."

Art admits that he is somewhat of a stickler for authenticity when it comes to performing his folk songs. For example,

*Art Thieme, folk singer and storyteller
(Larry Rand, photographer)*

he will improvise and adapt his program to a particular audience "by inserting humor, folk tales, puns, and whatever else it takes to get people to listen to music they're not familiar with, music that they don't hear on the radio." But, says the finicky folk singer, "I will not change the nature of my songs. They have been gleaned from libraries and mountain men across the country, and express a time and tradition that I respect, and I try to impart that to my listeners. It's like stepping into a time machine, with all the distractions of the era gone, and seeing only what the song wants you to see, talking about life in vivid, poetic terms. I see myself as a vehicle for the music."

If Art will not adapt his songs, neither will he succumb very often to writing his own material. "To me, writing my own folk songs would be like setting up an antique shop and putting a plastic table in the window."

The gist of Art's belief that folk music and its history have deep regional roots, and a special patina burnished by time, is captured in a comment made about his meeting with Clarence Mussehl: "He was a real find for me. All folk singers are used to learning from older people; that's where we have to go to find the old songs."

Tea and Saw

"I've never seen a real sawyer, only one on TV, and the first time was about seventeen years ago," says TATSUO HAMANO of Fukuoka, Japan. He plays the musical saw and banjo with his bluegrass group at "a very small tea room named The Villa. We decided to sing bluegrass songs translated into Japanese, folk songs and nursery rhymes, and enca (Japanese spirit songs). Naturally, the musical saw will help the show!"

Through several years of corresponding with Jim Leonard (whom Tatsuo calls *sensei*, meaning teacher), Hamano has indicated a desire to come to America to continue his studies in marine biology. But, he writes, "I didn't tell the most important reason: I want to touch the bluegrass traditional folk music. And I will never go to America without my saw and banjo."

Tatsuo Hamano (with saw) and Yasuo Miyoshi

TOSHITAKA ONOE, an employee of the Tokyo branch of the Chase Manhattan Bank, finds that "the musical saw matches well with the traditional oriental melodies of Japan, Korea, China, and other Southeast Asian countries." Onoe has sawed since 1976, following, he says, "an opportunity to hear Ichiro Sato play in Tokyo."

Toshitaka, who lives in Yokohama, plays a Sandvik "Stradivarius." He also imports Sandvik saws for distribution through the Friend Musical Instrument Shop, which is located in the shopping arcade of Tokyo Central Station.

Toshitaka Onoe (in jacket, importer of Sandvik musical saws) and Yoshizo Takano (owner of the Friend Musical Instrument Shop, Tokyo, Japan)

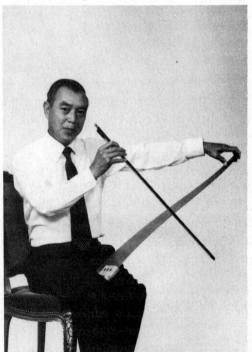

Toshitaka Onoe

Ripsawngs

DON FRANK plays an eight-point ripsaw whose brand he no longer remembers. "At one time it had a stamp on the face of the saw, but I never paid any attention to it. All I remember is that it said 'Musical Saw.'" A major point in the saw's favor, according to Don, is its flexibility, "which provides smooth, easy playing. Also, the left thumb is not taxed as much as if one were playing a 'stiff' saw. Its greatest weakness is a tendency to rust."

Don remembers seeing a number of sawyers on television programs from the time he was very young. "It seemed to me that the visual aspect of their performances far outweighed any sounds produced by sawing. The players often weren't very good and their intonation left much to be desired. I think the audience was just amazed that anyone could even produce a sound resembling music from the saw.

"I became interested in the musical saw when I was thirteen or fourteen [about 1966] after hearing the late Foster Baker play; he had been my father's Boy Scout leader. I'd had some experience with the violin and string bass, and the idea of learning to play a novelty instrument suddenly appealed to me, so I grabbed at the chance to learn anything I could from Mr. Baker."

Don learned his lessons well, and has performed in over a hundred cities in the United States. As a featured soloist in 1980 with the U.S. Air Force Band and Singing Sergeants, he appeared at Opryland U.S.A. in Nashville, Tennessee, and played a saw obligato while a tenor sang "All Around the Water Tank."

*William L. Ormandy
(Allan J. de Lay, photographer)*

Festival of the Saws, Santa Cruz, 1982 (Allan J. de Lay, photographer)

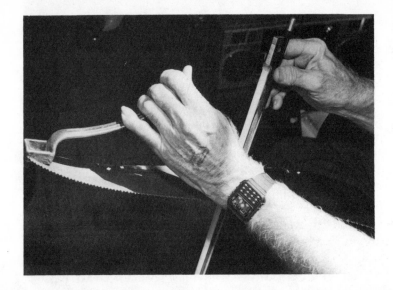

Frank Russell's tip grip (Allan J. de Lay, photographer)

Festival of the Saws, Santa Cruz, 1983 (Allan J. de Lay, photographer)

Like Father, Like Son

JAMES WINCHESTER WALLACE comes by his sawing honestly. "My Dad and I shared a lot of time and interests together, so when he began to play, I soon followed suit," says the youngest son of Dan Wallace.

"I probably saw my first saw player on a 'Gilligan's Island' episode, but the first sawyer I distinctly remember was my dad."

As one might expect, Jim now plays his father's musical saw. While an undergraduate student at Marquette University, he tested its sound production in his physics class. "The vibrations of the blade set up sound waves just like a guitar string does, and I found they are nearly perfect sine waves [indicating nearly perfect tone]."

Jim has spent the last several years earning a degree and graduated from the Illinois College of Optometry in 1988, the same year he attended the second annual International Musical Saw Festival and Saw-Off in Northridge, California, as a representative for Mussehl & Westphal. "I'm still an active sawyer," he says, "and I look forward to enjoying it for many years. Once I get settled in my career I'll take over more of Mussehl & Westphal's operations"

New Vaudeville

Imagine a single evening's show that includes comedy, singing, tap dancing, juggling, mime, musical groups, and magical feats.

It's the old vaudeville bill, right?

Wrong! It's the new vaudeville, and the Blue Sky Serenaders —JOEL ECKHAUS, BAU GRAVES, and LINDA PERVIER —are a talented Maine trio mining the sounds and styles of the '20s, '30s and '40s.

"Vaudeville is definitely on the rise around here," says Eckhaus, who regularly astonishes audiences with his accomplished performances on the musical saw. With Linda doing vocals, Bau on guitar or accordion, and Joel on the saw (or maybe the mandolin, ukulele, or banjo), the trio strums the gamut of American popular music from ragtime to rock, Dixieland to doo-wopp, jazz, instrument novelties, and vaudeville songs.

"I don't recall ever seeing a saw player before I learned to play," Joel says, "but my roommate could imitate the sound of a saw with her voice. She sent away for a saw, and while she was at work, I read the instructions and learned to play. That was about about 1977 or 1978. The first sawyer I met was John Hunt, then of Bath, Maine."

In his musical travels, Joel has dug up a bit of saw history —scarce as hen's teeth and much more welcome. He studied string instruments with the vaudevillian Roy Smeck, known as the "Wizard of the Strings," who was still active in 1983 as a teacher and performer in New York City, according to a 1983 article in *Sweet Potato*. Joel writes that "Roy has an old 78 rpm record (possibly Victor), of sawist Sam Moore playing 'That Old Pal of Mine.' It's

Blue Sky Serenaders, (from left) Joel Eckhaus, Linda Pervier, Bau Graves

one of Roy's first recordings; he plays guitar, probably around 1921. [Smeck] claims it is the first saw recording ever made, and he also says that the instrument in Paul Whiteman's recording of 'Whispering' is not a musical saw, as many people think, but a slide whistle."

In a postscript, Eckhaus adds, "In North Conway, New Hampshire, there is a man who runs a music store (there's only one in town), who has photos of his father's dance band in Leipzig, Germany, circa 1928, in which [the father] played drums and 'singing saw.' The saws were displayed on the front of the bass drum."

Not content to simply apply themselves to neo-vaudeville, the chameleonic Blue Sky Serenaders change costumes and become part of The Howitzers, said to be "the only live mandolin orchestra north of Boston." Twenty-one straight-faced, bow-tied, mostly bearded musicians perform under the baton of Maestro Bau Graves.

P.S. Linda is beribboned, not bearded, and apparently wows audiences with her superb scat singing.

Speaking of The Howitzers, the group includes JOHN HUNT, "who adds to the distinction of being a Howitzer that of being the highest ranking saw player in the U.S. Navy" (*Sweet Potato*, 1983).

John's sister bought him a musical saw in 1971, "but I saw my first sawyer long before that on Ted Mack's 'The Original Amateur Hour,' when I was a kid."

Besides sawing with The Howitzers, John has played at the Maine Festival for years, the New Jersey Folk Festival, and miscellaneous fairs and other musical events on the East Coast.

When John is not sawing or navying, he is writing humor, and he has given us permission to share with you excerpts from his essay entitled "An Erudite Exposition Concerning the History of the Musical Saw" (copyright 1983 by John West Hunt):

> The earliest authenticated reference to the musical saw is recorded in Biblical text. Recent archaeological finds have confirmed that early religious music was written for close three-part harmony for the three sizes of saw: Large (L), Medium (M), and Small (S). This accounts for the naming of the Old Testament's collection of songs, Book of Psalms, a translational variation of the original name, SAWLMS. . . . In the late nineteenth century, the little known but up-and-coming-Austrian neurologist and amateur saw player, Sigmund Freud, ensured his place in history by using the saw in his early work in psychoanalysis. He has been credited with inventing the complementary fret and coping saws which have proven to be invaluable tools for do-it-yourself psychoanalysts. . . . Amazingly, many Americans still believe that sharps are played on the toothy side of the saw; [that] hacksaws are used either by mediocre saw players, taxicab drivers, or naval officers restricted to quarters; and [that] circular saws are used to play rounds. None of that is true, of course. . . . It should also be noted that obvious references to sawhorses and seesaws (sometimes confused with sea saws used by sailors and with C-saws), not in keeping with the intellectual tenor of this essay, have been avoided but can be found in elementary texts of this subject.

And on that note, we say "sawyonara" to John Hunt of Red Bank, New Jersey.

"The Whistling Brakeman" toots in from Calgary, Alberta, Canada. ROY THORESON took up the instrument in 1980, after hearing another Calgarian, Frank Megill, play at a party. In 1983, Roy auditioned his saw act for a telethon and was accepted. Since then he is a regular performer at the world-known annual Calgary Stampede, and he has played on many TV variety shows, at clubs, at the Santa Cruz Festival of the Saws, and at the International Musical Saw Festival and Saw-Off in Northridge, California. The silver-haired Roy is generally accompanied by Bark-N-Saw Traveler, an unusual mutt, who, although he does not whistle, often manages to steal Roy's saw act.

The Whistling Brakeman (Roy Thoreson), with Bark-N-Saw Traveler (Allan J. de Lay, photographer)

Double the Pleasure

For tree surgeon LARRY HANLEY, his trusty saw is more than just another tool of the trade. When Larry finishes his day's work, he simply turns the saw around and plays the night away.

When Larry first contacted us he apologized for being late with his correspondence because he had been "up country." We are not sure where that is from Larry's hometown of Nambour, Queensland, Australia, but it must be a hunk of miles because his letter is postmarked three months after our initial contact.

All levity aside, Larry notes, "There are a few sawyers in Australia, but it is not easy to get on to them. Most often they are bushmen who just tinker with it and often have never heard of using a bow."

Just thirteen years old when he heard the saw played for the first time at an outdoor concert, Larry says, "I marvelled at the beautiful sound such a humble instrument could produce. That was to haunt me for nearly twenty years. I'd often think about it and sometimes try to imitate the sound of a saw while whistling, but was never able to catch on to how it really worked."

Larry tried to play a handsaw or two, "but I found them stiff and uncooperative for a beginner. I decided I simply must have a go at this and ordered a saw from Fort Atkinson, which, with freight and import duty was the most expensive saw I've ever purchased!"

Now, having played since 1981 before senior citizen groups —"a real walk down memory lane for them" —and similar organizations, our Australian sawyer feels he is ready to tackle television. He has also been experimenting with amplified saw sounds, using "a number of cheap K-Mart saws. I feel the scope for an amplified saw is almost unlimited."

Utaroku Miyakoya, Tokyo, Japan

Jack I. Arons, circa 1950's

He has the friendly look-alike face of actor Karl Malden. We know him as "Cousin Ernie." More formally, he is ERNEST W. PEISKER, a Chicago-area sawyer who "saw a fella hammer a tune in '79 in Steamboat Springs, Colorado."

Since 1982, "Cousin Ernie" (who jokes that his saw playing cuts into his banjo time) employs alternately a cello bow and a xylophone mallet on his saws, a 28-inch C. Black-lock Special and a 28-inch Mussehl & Westphal.

His enthusiasm for the instrument extends beyond music-making. Pictured below is Peisker's handmade "coat of arms," a crossed musical saw and banjo fashioned into a belt buckle.

"Cousin Ernie" (Ernest W. Peisker)

The miniature saw handle is wood and the blade is steel. The "beheaded" banjo turned out to be no joke. Ernie writes, "One day my saw fell over and landed teeth first onto my mylar plastic banjo head and cut a two-inch-long gash."

Ernest W. Peisker's handmade belt buckle

"I remember well my grandfather saying, many years ago, that in his homeland, the Canary Islands, Spain, there were sawyers," WILLIAM ALEMAN says. "He was a cabinet-maker and we had saws of all kinds and sizes around the house. I vaguely recall that as a small boy I used to hit those saws to make them sound."

A resident of the small island of Puerto Rico, Aleman's first exposure to a sawyer was an Adventist pastor from Haiti, "whose name was Napoleon Charles. He played Christian hymns on the saw with a violin bow. Although it sounded well, I knew something was missing."

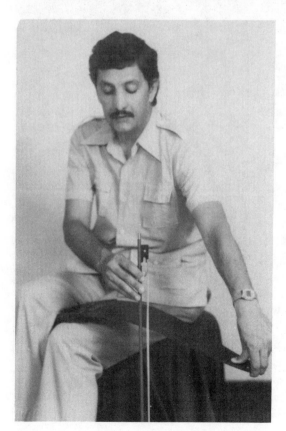

A year later, in Mayaguez, while studying theology, Aleman heard a schoolmate from Cuba, Eliezer Barreiro, play the musical saw. "His interpretation of the hymn 'The Holy City' was masterful in tone, skill, ability and expression. This friend was my first and only teacher and I consider him a great sawyer. He is now a pastor in Brooklyn, New York."

Within a year's time of purchasing his saw (an Atkins #1000 with a plastic handle, in 1963), Aleman was playing in social and religious activities. "I can perform sacred music, popular and classical, but I prefer opera arias. My repertoire includes works by composers such as Verdi, Bizet, Donizetti, Bellini, and so forth."

William Aleman

Ninety Plus

Rumors whisper that he is ninety if a day, but no one really knows how old CLYDE DAWSON is —and he won't tell. But we know by his own admission that he still has his father's violin, which is over one hundred years old; that he met the Weavers on the Orpheum vaudeville circuit during the 1920s; and that for fifty-four years he corresponded with Clarence Mussehl, of whom he says: "A great guy. Hope he is enjoying his visit with the Heavenly Hosts among the fleecy clouds."

A little jive always peppers his talk, ya dig? And he swings rapidly from one subject to another, not waiting for an answer, maybe not even expecting one. Occasionally, his wife, Louise (she plays the spoons and Clyde taught her musical sawing) tries to round out the information by a well-planted question.

A chuckle gurgles in Clyde's throat and his eyes twinkle as he tosses out bits and pieces of yesteryear, so you know he has been cutting up for quite some time. But there are never enough details for the listener to stitch together a whole canvas of Clyde Dawson's experience —sort of like the irregular, colorful cloth scraps that Louise is stitching into a crazy quilt. That's the way Clyde likes it, and who would try to change one of sawing's venerable golden oldies?

(From left) Louise Dawson, Jim Leonard, Clyde Dawson, March 1984 (Janet E. Graebner, photographer)

*Clyde Dawson, March 1984
(Jim Leonard, photographer)*

Whatever Clyde's age, you won't find him and Louise at their Anaheim home if the wanderbug bites, and it often does. Then they load their California camper and hit the road, lugging along their saws, bones and spoons, and any number of other "musical" instruments, some of which Clyde invented: a bass horn, bass dulcimer, and a musical shovel, for example.

Clyde purchased his first professional musical saw in 1924, he says, "for about seven dollars —the whole works: saw, rosin, bow, everything —from an ad in *Mechanics Illustrated*. But Louise and I don't use professional musical saws anymore. The controversy is settled as far as we're concerned [whether a professional musical saw or a hardware handsaw plays better]. We switched when I found two commercial saws we could both play. The tone is just as good."

Sometimes, in lieu of the highways and byways, they do more exotic things, like riding river rafts down the Colorado River. Or taking a slow boat to Hawaii: a 1980 trip on the Independence, playing with the Hawaiian Trio. Or floating along on a Southern river boat: their act was booked in 1977 on the Mississippi Delta Queen.

The Dawsons also keep in tune with various kitchen bands and a thirty-piece orchestra, The Syncopators, that plays old-time melodies and nostalgic fox trots, waltzes and tangos. And Clyde demonstrated that he can still hoof a mean cakewalk.

In the 1930s, Clyde's group, The Missourians, using homemade instruments, entertained professionally in the midwest states. Referring to this period in a 1971 letter to Clarence Mussehl, Clyde said, "Your saw instrument was the main attraction. . . . I'm glad to know that you are still vibrating from the same address. I'll keep sawing away for my own amusement until I greet Peter at the Golden Gate, and if He doesn't admit me, I'll sneak around to the side and saw my way through the fence." [Editor's note: See Appendix C.]

Will the day ever come when Suzy cannot go out to play because she is practicing the saw? ELLIS TRAUB of Boca Raton, Florida, hopes so. He believes the saw has been "stereotyped as eerie and whining, and its function usually reserved for hillbilly bands." Since his retirement in 1973, Ellis has endeavored to further the public's appreciation of what he calls "a bona fide musical instrument capable of producing a wide range of sounds. I'm enjoying my 'second career' as a musical saw artist more actively than ever."

A sawyer for over sixty years, Ellis initially heard a 1920s vaudeville saw played in Yonkers, New York. "Then one day while passing a musical instrument store in New York City, I noticed a saw on display in the window. . . . I left the store with a cardboard box tucked under my arm, the proud possessor of a carpenter's saw and a single six-inch-square piece of literature, the instructions. . . . Alas, no one could show me how to play it."

Unlike his accomplished cello playing, Ellis's struggles to saw music initially produced "only howling noises, ghostly whines, and perhaps similar vibrations from neighbors." Continued determination prevailed, however, and he realized he was making progress when his wife started to recognize simple, familiar melodies. Both agreed that "the worst was over."

Through the years, cruising along the eastern seaboard states, playing before amazed audiences, Traub feels that he has "conducted sort of a one-man crusade to preserve a lost art."

Though the musical saw may never replace Suzy's piano, Ellis emphasizes that it has economical advantages as well as being durable. "There's nothing to wear out here, unless your pants get caught in the saw blade."

The Whistling Saw

PHILIP W. MINER was "not aroused," he says, at age thirteen when he heard a sawyer at the Gladwin Theatre on Jefferson Avenue near Waterworks Park in Detroit, Michigan.

But fourteen years later, in 1935, when he was a member of a minstrel act sponsored by a businessmen's club in Detroit, he heard the president of a lumber company play the saw. "This sparked my interest," Phil admits. He bought not one but two saws the next day. "Unfortunately, there was no one to even give me a hint on how to bend it. Now comes the payoff!! After about four months of concentrated practice, I learned that the saw player at the minstrel show was not actually playing the saw; he was only going through the motions and whistling the tune!"

Phil still uses his early 1930-vintage saw, which is stamped Broadcasting Musical Saw, with a picture of an old-fashioned microphone etched on it. "I never did know the brand name. As for the second saw purchased at the same time, it has long been relegated to my tool cabinet —can't depend on the tones. Today, I would recommend the Nicholson 300, available at hardware stores, or some of the Swiss saws, which play well because of the excellent metal used in them."

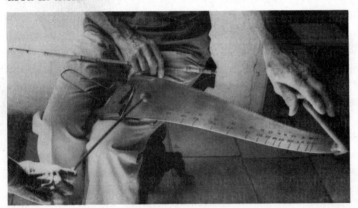

Musical scale markings on Phil Miner's saw

Phil Miner

Phil has marked the musical scale on his blade, which serves as a teaching device; and he markets two accessories that he has invented to aid sawyers, "so they can concentrate on playing rather than continually fighting the saw." One is a tone-control handle fastened to the tip end (similar to the lever on the French *lame sonore*), which Phil says allows for a better grip and alleviates the tired-fingers syndrome; the other is a lap support, which prevents the saw from slipping between the sawyer's knees. He also makes his own bows out of bamboo from his backyard in Santa Ana, California, and he offers printed instructions on bow making (but you will probably have to find your own bamboo).

Dividing his time each year between Santa Ana and San Juan, Puerto Rico, Phil has had ample time during the past "forty-eight years plus" to perform in both places, including frequent appearances on Puerto Rican television: "Pacheco's Famous Children" and pianist Papio Paz's TV show, "Pianissimo."

"There are many references to the saw in the King James version of the Old Testament,"

Phil notes. "One that comes to mind is Isaiah 10:15: 'Shall the saw magnify itself against him that shaketh it?' We saw players do shake our saws in different ways! It seems quite appropriate, when we play hymns on our musical saws, that the best known carpenter who came out of Bethlehem should be praised on his own instrument."

The saw is only one of more than *eighty* world-wide ethnic instruments in the collection of Canadian RANDY RAINE-REUSCH, and he plays all of them.

The Vancouver, British Columbia, resident is an instrumentalist, choreographer, composer, and registered massage therapist, who has spent the last several years integrating his musical resources with a variety of seminars, workshops, and individual programs in the fields of self-awareness and holistic healing.

Randy lists the musical saw as a "secondary instrument, often played with synthesizers and computers when I perform contemporary and experimental music. And I also use the saw in some of my compositions for contemporary dance."

Despite Randy's talent on the musical saw, however, from among his many instruments it was the glass harmonica that caught our attention, for two reasons. First, because the sound of the musical saw has often been compared to this fragile instrument. Second, Clarence Mussehl sold a similar instrument under the name Glass-O-Phone, which was featured in his group, The Maestro's Harmonizers.

Randy's music literature indicates that the glass harmonica was developed over 300 years ago, although its exact origins are unknown. "It gained popularity in Europe, especially Germany, until it was banned for 'medical' reasons, such as: causing young men to faint, reviving young women from a faint, curing gout, and cleansing the blood." Two women performers apparently went insane, yet "even with the problems, the instrument's music was so beautiful that Beethoven and Mozart both composed for it and Anton Mesmer (the father of hypnotism) used it in his work."

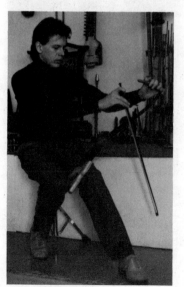

Randy assures us that he is not suffering any ill effects from playing his century-old glass harmonica. Consisting of thirty-six wine glasses tuned to perfect pitch (five were replaced twenty years ago), the instrument is mounted on a wooden sound board and the glasses are held in place by leather brackets. By running his moistened fingers around the rims of the glasses, which have been filled with varying amounts of water, Randy creates a vibration that produces the desired musical tone.

Randy Raine-Reusch, with his musical saw and other instruments (Xaliman, photographer)

The Frozen North

North to Alaska was IKE W. KUSISTO's motto in 1928. "I was going to organize an Alaskan Eskimo dance band, but my timing was bad. It was during the depression and the wrong time to take the orchestra on the road." So Ike went to work for the Juneau Mining Company and spent more than two decades in Alaska. He finally returned to the United States in 1951 and formed two companies for mining development and consulting.

Although Ike's plans for an Eskimo dance band were coldly received, he was asked in 1931 to play saw solos at the governor's mansion in Juneau. "I dug out my saw to practice and found it was all rusty from the damp, salty air. So I went to the hardware store and asked the owner if I could try out his saws for tone. After about a dozen saws, I found one to have the best tone of any saw I ever had, and it was the least expensive saw, about $2.75. The brand name was Bear Cub or something like that."

A newspaper clipping about the music program that evening at the governor's mansion describes how "the ordinary hand-saw as a musical instrument made its initial appearance in Juneau, and the novelty of the thing took the audience by storm."

Postscript: Maybe the mystery of Phil Miner's "unknown brand" for his 1930-era Broadcasting Musical Saw is solved. Of the three saws Ike Kusisto now plays, he mentions a 26-inch blade that is marked Broadcasting Model Musical Saw, from Mussehl & Westphal.

Ike Kusisto

In the Picture

Photographer ALLAN J. de LAY, of Portland, Oregon, observes, "I take pictures for pay, but I play the saw for enjoyment. It's an outlet. The only time I've played for pay was when I was with the military." That would have been his stint with the "Artic Antics," a U.S. Air Force Special Services entertainment troupe that performed for seven months in Alaska and the Aleutians during 1943.

As a ten-year old in Topeka, Kansas, in 1925, Allan saw his first so-called sawyer, a carpenter who was making weird sounds by striking his saw with a stick. Allan was intrigued, but not enough to take up musical sawing until 1930, after his family had already moved to Oregon.

The Great Depression dictated that he find whatever work he could and at sixteen he was a delivery boy for a dental supply firm. In the company's basement, de Lay found an old handsaw hanging on the wall and spent most of his lunch hours banging at it with a mallet, trying to match the tunes he heard on the radio. He soon purchased his own saw, he says, "and I performed a lot for free meals. That was really something then —those were hard times."

Allan J. de Lay (John Denny, photographer)

Six months later, "My mother bought a used musical saw from a neighbor for ten dollars worth of dressmaking—a bronze or gold-plated one with sparkler 'jewels' in the carved handle." Fifty-one years later at the 1982 Festival of the Saws in Santa Cruz —"I'd never met more than two sawyers before then" — Allan learned that his gold-plated saw, which he still plays, is a prized Mussehl & Westphal model.

Staff sergeant Allan J. de Lay, U.S. Air Force, Special Services Show Troupe ("Artic Antics"), 1943, Alaska and the Aleutian Islands

Allan gave up his hammering ways in 1941 when he started playing for radio broadcasts at the Army Air Force Base in Portland. The program director said the mallet made too harsh a sound for radio transmission, so Allan switched to a violin bow. Today, he uses a fiberglass 3/4 violin bow with nylon strings.

Allan's foreign travel is phenomenal; far too many places to name them all. At each stop he unsheaths his saw and gives concerts: Europe, Canada, the United States, Mexico, Hawaii, South America, Japan, Africa, India, ad infinitum. Since 1973, he has kept a record of his events, logging nearly 600 performances.

His collection of tapes and early recordings goes back as far as 1937, and he joined Dick Fagan in 1954 on some of the first television programming in the Oregon area. He was a guest soloist with the Oregon Symphony in 1974, playing the saw solo in Aram Khachaturian's "Concerto for Piano and Orchestra." In 1979, at the World Scout Jamboree in Sweden, Allan dedicated a song to King Carl Gustav, who remembered him two years later when he made a royal visit to a National Scout Jamboree in Virginia and designated de Lay the official "court photographer."

Allan also teamed up with banjoist Eddie Peabody for several shows in the early 1960s, and he gave some "fine points in sawing" to the celebrated violinist, Yehudi Menuhin, who was curious about Allan's instrument.

With more than a half-century of sawyership behind him, it would seem that de Lay had done just about everything worth sawing. But no, as a musician, he says, "I have one major desire remaining. I would love someday to play 'Ave Maria' with a church organ accompanist."

It has been said there is no such thing as a native Californian, but ROBERT ARMSTRONG claims otherwise, being "a native Californian originally from Pasadena."

Now living in northern California, Bob has been playing saw since 1968, when he met a farmer named Madsen in Kerteminde, Fyn, Denmark. His familiarity with the musical saw occurred much earlier, however, through 78 rpm recordings and animated films from the 1930s.

Over the years, Bob writes, "I've performed and recorded with various groups which feature vintage dance music of the teens, twenties and thirties: the Rural Sophisticates (including an appearance on television's 'PM Magazine'), The Yolano Novelty Orchestra, and the Cheap Suit Serenaders, plus radio shows in the Los Angeles and Sacramento area, and the nationally syndicated 'Dr. Demento Show.'"

Robert Armstrong

The Cheap Suit Serenaders, (clockwise) Robert Armstrong (with saw), Bob Brozman, Allan "Aldo" Dodge, Terry "Sharky" Zwigoff, Tony Marcus (contributed by Robert Armstrong)

Additional saw sounds from Bob can be heard with his own group, Armstrong's Pasadenians; on animated films by Sally Cruikshank and Michael McMillan; and as the introductory and closing theme music in the 1975 film "One Flew Over the Cuckoo's Nest."

Armstrong uses a German-style bass violin bow on his Sandvik "Stradivarius" baritone saw, a tenor M & W, and a C. Blacklock Special. "I like each of them for their respective tonal ranges and brilliance. All are made of good, flexible steel with a long blade design and a good taper for the best possible range."

Let 'er Rip

Saw players who manipulate huge two-man saws are a rare breed, or shy —or both. We know of only two: ripsaw player Bill Heier of San Francisco (see Chapter 5) and CHARLES W. HARDY, who "stands up" to his unwieldy tool. "I located a two-man crosscut saw and find it's flexible enough to hammer to get sound, and I tried my bow on it with encouraging results."

"Heads will roll" is not a statement to take lightly around Charles and his fierce-looking six-foot saw. "I was inspired to try it because of the fellow [Heier] who was able to play one at the 1983 Saw Festival."

Charles plays more than the crosscut, though, which is a new endeavor for him. In his "saw corral," he has "a couple of 14-inch antique saws from an uncle's basement that play beautifully, but in a limited range. They are rather difficult to play because the bowing area is so small and the notes must be carefully placed for the best tone. I've also purchased two cheap saws —a $3.95 26-inch, 8-point Stanley #39-300, and a $4.77 26-inch, 8-point Great Neck #PS26S —that play nearly as well as my professionally built ones. I also own two of Charlie Blacklock's saws; the 26-inch produces good tone and can be played quite loud. The 30-inch plays a few notes lower than other saws and is flexible enough for easy playing. It's a little long to use comfortably, though, and the range is not as uniform as my 1980 Mussehl & Westphal."

The musical saw that Hardy learned on was purchased, he explains, "five years before my birth, a gold-plated M & W. An aunt had bought it in 1920 and never learned to play it. She gave it to my father, her brother, who was a minister in the Baptist church. He played it sometimes in church services. I began trying to make sounds on it after I'd learned to whistle, between age eleven and twelve; thereafter, I had many opportunities to play during junior high and high school, in church, and socially in Elmira, New York."

Now, fifty-some years later, in Dearborn Heights, Michigan, Hardy says he occasionally still uses the gold saw. "Most of the gold has worn off and the copper undercoat shows, but the 'jewels' are still intact. The saw produces excellent tones, although it's limited in range and somewhat stiff."

An Irish Busker

HENRY DAGG'S first public appearance as a sawyer, at the 1987 International Musical Saw Festival and Saw-Off in Northridge, California, garnered him a first-place win in the traditional songs category. Traveling over five thousand miles from Belfast, Northern Ireland, his trip was financed by the British Broadcasting Corporation (BBC), with the understanding that Henry would record the festival, then edit and produce a program for BBC radio.

("Clutching at Saws" aired in Europe during November and December 1987, and "represents three months of solid slogging," Henry said. Tapes of the three-hour program are available from Jim Leonard, P.O. Box 2183, Santa Ana, CA 92707. Proceeds are donated to the International Musical Saw Festival, to promote the art of musical sawing.)

Henry's second public performance was as a busker (a British term for street entertainer) at the Fountain Centre shopping mall in Belfast, during the 1987 Christmas season. "It seemed a pity to let Christmas go by without trying out such an unusual instrument on the street," Henry said, "and I didn't do badly in contributions, either." The money helped to pay for a holiday in Australia and Henry's trip to the California saw festival in 1988.

The Dublin-born Dagg (in his early thirties and a sound engineer for the BBC since 1974) was trained from an early age on the piano and cello. These instruments were later superseded by the electric bass and various keyboard instruments, and Henry's interest in combining electronics and unusual sound effects.

Dagg's first original composition, in 1982, included the sounds of fire engine sirens, air horns, and gunshots. "Trimphony no. 1" (a symphony for telephones) followed in 1983. "The Kitchen Symphony" (played entirely on kitchen utensils) came out in 1985, and "Fanfare for the Bogey Man" (using train sounds) was composed in 1986, the same year the BBC asked Henry to arrange a Bach fugue, using any sounds he liked, for a radio program.

Arranging "Counterpoint no. 9, a Bach Fugue" was Henry's introduction to the musical saw. "I decided initially to use a wine glass for the two upper registers and a jew's-harp for the bottom two, but discovered the jew's-harp wasn't suitable for the tenor part, so I chose a car horn for tenor and used the harp for the bass. When I found the horn in an antique shop, the owner suggested a saw as another useful sound, so I bought a bow and tried out one of my workshop saws. It took awhile, but I finally got the one long note I needed to work into the fugue."

Having gotten that far, Henry said, "I spent some months searching for a good playable saw and found only one suitable maker, Tyzak & Turner, of Sheffield, England."

Soon after purchasing his saw, he heard about a sawyer in Ulster, the late Kevin Cunningham, who had Jim Leonard's brochure, which was forwarded to Henry. Since then, it is not unusual for Jim to receive calls from Belfast any time during the day or night —Henry's day, Jim's night.

Henry Dagg, International Musical Saw Festival and Saw-Off, 1987 (Adam Leonard, photographer)

Dear Jim,

Until I was seventy years young I didn't know there was such a thing as a musical saw. Then I spent one week with my son in northern Minnesota. One evening at the Waskish Baptist church, I heard David Leonhardt play his saw, and it was beautiful. He showed me how, and it looked so simple that I thought I could do it.

Finally, after much deliberation because of my age, I ordered one and received it sometime in February 1983. Most of the cats and dogs left the neighborhood because the screeching drove them crazy, but your tape correcting my mistakes was a great help, and now I can make music with the mallet, the dowel bow, and the string bow. But by far my best music is with the bass fiddle bow. . . . It seems wonderful to be able to draw a rosined bow across a saw, setting up vibrations that can be picked up by the human ear, producing beautiful music that's pleasing to hear.

I learned to play the saw for my own pleasure, but it seems as though other people enjoy hearing the music as well as I enjoy playing it, for they all want me to come back.

If an old man past seventy years of age can learn a new hobby in six months, and play it well enough to bring himself some relaxation, as well as pleasure to many others, then shame on you who say, "I just can't do it."

Your friend,
HENRY MENGES
Fort Myers, Florida

Yes, Virginia, There are Lady Sawyers

Are there any lady sawyers? I've never seen one, wrote a gentleman sawyer.

You bet your bow, Virginia! The men have no monopoly as accomplished saw musicians. The following ladies of our acquaintance would do June Weaver proud.

Starting at age six in Louisville, Kentucky, MARGARET DAVIS STEINBUCH performed from 1910 to 1918 as one of the Von-Daviess, a vaudeville song and dance act which also featured her older sisters, Regina and Loreana. The attractive youngsters sang and danced through forty states on the old Alex Pantages and Radio-Keith-Orpheum stage circuits until child labor laws ended Margaret's childhood career. "Nearly every show had a saw player," she told us, "and once you hear a musical saw, you never forget it. Believe me!"

In 1965 (years after her vaudeville days were over and after Margaret had become a professional violinist with the West Hills Music Club and the Cincinnati Symphony), she found a musical saw hanging on the wall of a music store. "I would love to try to play that!" she exclaimed, and the manager let her take it home. "But I couldn't get a sound from it."

Soon after, Margaret left to visit relatives in California, and one of their neighbors played the saw. "He gladly showed

Margaret (Davis) Steinbuch

me how to hold and bend it. Then he said, 'Go home and practice, practice, with your radio and so forth.' As a violinist with the West Hills Music Club, I had plenty of pianists to help me."

A reporter at the *Cincinnati Enquirer* once defined the sound from Margaret's saw as "both haunting and whiney; something akin to the sound of a captured mosquito in a Dixie cup held open-end to your ear." Such descriptions did not faze Margaret a bit as she racked up credits year after year. With her imitation leopard skin rifle case tucked under her arm, she was always ready to honor an invitation to play on her ten-dollar saw. "It's a beautiful sound and I love performing. I guess it's the ham in me. I really enjoyed the times I played as a soloist with the Cincinnati Symphony and on the Mississippi Delta Queen."

Margaret was being modest. Add to the above: the "Gary Moore Show" at Rockefeller Center, the National Federation of Music Clubs Convention, the home for retired motion picture actors in California, numerous veterans' hospitals, county fairs, community clubs, the Santa Cruz Saw Festival, and radio and television appearances. One of her "most fun" impromptu performances, she said, occurred on another visit to California.

It was Christmas 1974, Margaret related, "I was at my daughter Joan's home in Burbank. Some remodeling was being done to the house, and when the carpenter laid down his saw to go after some other tools, I snatched up my cello bow and began to play 'Silent Night.' The astonishment on his and other workers' faces was hilarious! He told me afterwards that he might never saw again with that 'delicate, beautiful instrument.' Not every carpenter's saw can be used as a musical saw, however. I was just fortunate that his could carry a tune."

Margaret, billed as the "boy" in the Von-Daviess vaudeville song and dance act, with sisters Loreana and Regina Davis, circa 1913 (contributed by Margaret Steinbuch)

Margaret's passion for the musical saw gradually superseded that for her violin, and from the late 1960s until her death in March 1984, Margaret became well known for her attempts to interest others in the instrument. The clique that grew up around her nicknamed her the "saw ambassador," which fit in with her role as the leader of an imaginary Society for the Preservation of the Musical Saw. "It's a folk art that will die out if nobody teaches it to our young people," she fretted. "If older people will teach their grandchildren the saw, it will go on and on." It was a commitment she put into practice by teaching her own granddaughter, Jessica Nelson, how to play. "I tell people if they can whistle or hum a tune they can learn to play the saw."

Copy of the letterhead used for the Von-Daviess vaudeville act, 1913 (contributed by Margaret Steinbuch)

Saw Much Determination

In 1969, DEBBIE "Singing Saw" BELLANTE begged her first sawyer, Clayton Templeton, a missionary from East Brazil, to show her how it worked. He did, then he loaned Debbie his saw. "I practiced for two straight days, stopping only for meals and bedtime at my folks' insistence," she says. "The first day, I could play a scale and two songs. By the end of the second day I was playing slow music."

Now a professional sawyer living in Killeen, Texas, Debbie has played at Knott's Berry Farm (Buena Park, California), on radio programs, and at folk music festivals in her home state of Wisconsin.

Her desire to play the musical saw does not surprise anyone who knows her, she says. "As a child, I wanted to play every instrument created. I got halfway through the brass section and mastered a couple of the strings (I played the viola in the Denver City and Omaha City orchestras), and I play the trombone, the accordion and the baritone harp. But after playing

Debbie "Singing Saw" Bellante

the musical saw, I settled on that. Once I learned how to play it I didn't have to practice, and you know how kids don't like to practice!"

Debbie's choice of instruments has caused her a few problems, especially when flying. "The case [a long, thin wood box] looks like a gun case. Once a gate attendant stopped me from boarding a plane, and even after I played my saw in the terminal he still wouldn't let me on."

Another incident sounds like it could have had more serious consequences. Debbie was living with her parents at a mission in Bogota, Columbia. "We had traveled two and a half days by boat up river to visit a remote Indian settlement. I never go anywhere for more than a couple of days without my saw, and when I brought it out and played it for the Indians, they thought it was devil music and reacted very strongly. Another tribe, however, just thought it was one of those strange things that missionaries do. Incidentally, most tribal natives believe missionaries have weird customs."

In 1986, a reporter described Debbie's saw as "the pleasant sound of a perfectly toned operatic soprano"; and, not surprisingly, she was once asked to play a singer's high notes in a cantata.

Not only does sawing make heavenly music for Debbie, it also introduced her to Anthony, who at the time they met was stationed at the U.S. Marine Corps Base at Camp Pendleton, Oceanside, California. Says Anthony, "I was at a music festival and some friends said to come and listen to this girl who was playing a saw. I couldn't believe it. I thought it was great and I had to meet her."

Debbie's greatest wish is to play with the Grand Ol' Opry, she revealed, and —like many of our sawyers —she believes in passing on her talent, but she is not waiting for grandchildren to do that. "Just as soon as my son, John, is old enough to hold a saw . . . "

MARIAN McDERMOTT traveled by Greyhound bus all the way from Deerfield, Illinois, to Santa Cruz, California, to hammer her M & W saw at the 1981 Saw Festival . . . then decided to sing Fannie Brice and Sophie Tucker songs rather than play her instrument in the amateur saw-off. She plays with a senior citizen group in Deerfield.

Marian McDermott

Summer of '44

"I guess it all began way back in the summer of 1944 in Wauwatosa, Wisconsin," recalls NANCY SPENCER. "I had just graduated from high school, and was working on the assembly line in a so-called defense plant to earn money for college. Into our neighborhood came George Nixon, a businessman who carried a saw with him on his travels. He was visiting across the street and amazed the neighborhood kids with his music. I happened to have a violin bow, so I started playing my father's Disston saw that very day. When I went off to college, I took it along. I doubt my father ever missed it."

Nancy Spencer

During her college days, Nancy played with a group called Full Spittoon and his Hour of Harm, a take-off, according to Nancy, on Phil Spitalny and his Hour of Charm, an all-girl radio orchestra popular in the late forties. "In addition to the saw, our instrumentation included the comb and toilet paper, shower hose, kazoo, harmonica, and a piano to hold us all together."

In 1963, Nancy moved from Wisconsin to Oregon, and some place along the line she lost her father's saw. "So I visited a local hardware, tried out all their saws, and chose another Disston —a Townsman, I think. In those days, if I could play 'Un Bel Di' from *Madame Butterfly* on a saw the range was acceptable."

In Nancy's journey towards the well-tempered sawyer, a major event occurred in 1970 in Copenhagen, she says, "when I found a Sandvik 'Stradivarius' hanging in a hardware store. I was thrilled with its two-octave range and beautiful rich, low notes." Returning to America, she added an M & W, "which is also two octaves and approximately a fourth higher in pitch than the Sandvik. Now I had a soprano and an alto saw."

During three decades of sawing, Nancy had never met another saw player. But that changed dramatically in 1974 when she accepted an engagement to the Expo '74 Folklife Festival in Spokane, Washington. "That first week at the Expo was unforgettable. I played more saw than I had in the entire thirty years leading up to it!" Her solitary sawyer status took on a new dimension as her credits grew from coast to coast: "A Prairie Home Companion" with Garrison Keillor, Santa Cruz Saw Festivals, Ken Kesey's Poetic Hoohaw, Spirit of '78 (Erie, Pennsylvania), Fox Hollow Folk Festival (Petersboro, New York), Musithon (Corvallis, Oregon), coffee houses, college festivals, a tour across Canada —and more.

Nancy's sawing events and wanderlust complement each other, so if you see a lady wearing Birkenstock sandals, and carrying a homemade leather case slung over her left shoulder —with a message on the back: It's a saw, I play it —say hi to Nancy.

(From left) Nancy Spencer, Tom Scribner, Allan J. de Lay, 1982

Return to Springfield

Springfield, Missouri. The historical starting point in 1904 for musical sawing by the Weavers: Leon, Frank, and June. And the home of GEORGIA BRUNNER, who at the age of nine first heard the musical saw played in her church. "I thought this must be heaven. I was so thrilled with it I vowed that someday I would play the saw. The man who played was so good that I felt chills run through me."

Georgia's saw studies were delayed, however, until 1979, at which time, she says, "My husband bought me a musical saw for my birthday, after I had met "Ramblin' Ray" Ricketts at a music and crafts festival at Silver Dollar City. I was so taken by Ray's playing and so excited that I introduced myself to him and I was on my way."

Four years later —"One year of sheer frustration and about three years that is somewhat pleasing to other people's ears" —Georgia now plays with a Grandmothers Club, a group of musicians that perform at hospitals and children's homes in Springfield.

Georgia Brunner

Not every sawyer has enough luck to scratch at the Sahara Club in Las Vegas, Nevada. "Of course, we had to audition first," says SARAH FOSTER. The "we" is Sarah and husband Maurice, who accompanies her on the piano. The "luck" was Foster's daughters, who were singing at the club in March 1983.

Like Georgia Brunner, Sarah was nine when she heard her first sawyer in the mid-thirties at her church. "I watched that man with his saw and mallet, then I went home intending to duplicate the sweet tones on my dad's tools. It didn't work."

Twenty-five years later, Foster says, "My ambition for musical sawing was resharpened when I read a mail order advertisement, and I sent off for the whole kit and kaboodle." Her family —Maurice and five children —did not take kindly at first to her endeavors. Sarah was banished to the bedroom along with their howling dog. Eventually, she won the dog's approval, and finally her family's, to play in the living room.

More than twenty years of practice since 1960 account for Sarah's improved sawing and appearances in Kansas (the Fosters live on a farm near Tribune), Oklahoma, Colorado, California, and Missouri, where she has a standing invitation to saw at Silver Dollar City.

Not only does Sarah stroke the saw, but she scratches the fiddle, toots the saxophone, and rattles the bones; a cow's rib bones, to be exact, which she holds in one hand and waves with a lazy S motion to produce a rhythmic clacking. Sarah stuffs them into her boots while playing the saw (either one of her two M & W's, a "Stradivarius," or a Stanley Handyman). Maurice designed a removable cherrywood cap that Sarah slips over the tip of her saw, "which sure saves wear and tear on my thumb, and provides better leverage."

Sarah (like some others) believes the theory that the musical saw, when compared to other musical instruments, has the most perfect tone. "Jim Turner, whom I have played saw duets with, had the saw tested on the oscilloscope at Denver University and it has the most perfect sine waves."

Some of Sarah's enthusiasm for musical sawing must have rubbed off on her family, because one of her sons plays, and a couple of grandchildren show an interest in learning. She insists that becoming a sawyer isn't all that difficult. "With a good teacher, a person could cut months of labor off the learning process, and maybe not have to spend so much time in the bedroom. The dog might even settle down after a few days!"

Sarah Foster (with musical bones tucked in her left boot) and husband Maurice

"I heard a woman from Henderson play while I was touring an antique house," reports LILLIAN PULLEN of Council Bluffs, Iowa. "I thought it made beautiful music." That was in January 1983 and Lillian bought her saw soon afterwards. The following March, she told Jim Leonard that

Myrtle Mizell

she had "finally found the high notes on the saw, but I still hear the grating. I get frustrated at times because I want to learn so bad. I've done everything but sit on the bow to get rid of the bothersome bow noise. It's getting better and other people can't hear it, but I can."

The last we heard, Lillian had progressed to the point of playing two-part harmony duets with another lady sawyer; again proving the old saw that practice makes perfect.

Dorothy J. Farmer with Tom Scribner, 1982

Kate Wolfe (guitar) and Victoria Bolam, 1983 (Allan J. de Lay, photographer)

In a brief note, DOROTHY J. FARMER says, "I purchased my saw in February 1982 and had difficulty learning to play on my own. Then I met Mr. [Tom] Scribner and he showed me how to hold it. He wasn't feeling well that day and was very nervous."

Sawing Seeds Abroad

"Heard a boy play a saw just once, the year I graduated from college in 1921," writes ninety-two-year-old HAZEL S. LAWSON, who has been sawing musically for over sixty years. "I was married, so my husband and I went to the Atkins Saw Works at Indianapolis and we bought a crosscut and a ripsaw and started practicing. We both used violin bows and always played with our bows going in the same direction, like violinists. If we had a pause, we would each drop our bow down and start again with an 'up' bow."

Hazel left her home in Battle Creek, Michigan, to travel abroad, sowing the seeds of sawing wherever she went. "I've been clear around the world twice and have played the saw in many foreign countries, and have taught so many how to play it. Later, I'd send them a professional musical saw as a gift —I've bought at least twenty-five saws —and many of those students have become good saw players. Some were missionaries on islands that had no musical instruments and they were so glad to have one to accompany a choir."

According to Hazel, even remote islanders display some apprehension when they see rifle-shaped cases. She mentions a Chinese friend, Danny Oh, who was visiting in Borneo, "when the police saw him with this 'weapon' and took him to the police station. While he was waiting to be interviewed, he got his saw out and started playing it, and everyone came in to see what they were hearing. Needless to say, they let him go."

Noteworthy

ELFRIEDE HABLÉ started studying the saw in 1947 at age thirteen, after a music professor at the Horak Music Conservatory in Vienna, Austria —frustrated at Elfriede's refusal to learn notes —gave her his Feldmann saw (now more than 108 years old), saying, "You don't have to learn notes if you can play that thing! But you have to have great musical understanding."

Undaunted, and with great musical understanding, Elfriede adapted her natural music ability to perfecting her musical saw techniques. Over the years, she has appeared at the Salzburg Festival and toured in Europe with the James Last Orchestra, and played on numerous talent shows and television programs, including "Was sehen Sie?" (What Do You Say?) with Peter Hey; Heinz Conrad's "Guten Abend am Samstag" (Good Evening on Saturday); and the London-based British Broadcasting Corporation's "Cliff Richard Show."

Elfriede Hablé, Vienna, Austria

Saucy Sawyer

The Saw-C-Lady from Santa Ana, California, PATRICIA GRAHAM, is more careful of her choice of words these days. Learning to play the saw started out as a joke, which she expected to be soon forgotten.

The tale: In 1980 she and a friend dressed like Minnie and Mickey Mouse and put on roller skates, and wowed the audience gathered for the annual Garden Grove United Methodist's annual ice cream social. Of this rollicking, rolling routine, Pat exclaims, "I'm not young, you know!"

Asked repeatedly how she was going to top that act, Pat flippantly said, "Oh, some year I'll play my musical saw."

Uh, oh. "I don't know where that came from. The good Lord must have put it into my head because I didn't know a thing about musical saws."

The sequel: "I was caught in my own mousetrap! After that, every year before the church social, someone would ask, 'When are you going to play your musical saw?'"

Finally, baited by a friend for not "sawing to it that she kept a promise," Pat bought a hardware saw and one of Phil Miner's bamboo bows strung with nylon fishline. Beginning in October 1984, she studied musical sawing with Phil, until he moved away (Pat assures us his leaving had nothing to do with her sawing). Now she sits in on Jim Leonard's Monday night saw jams ("Pat plays real good saw," he says), and she makes up part of the trio that includes

Jim and Frank Holley. In 1987, they played together in a music video with the rock group "Kansas" and on KNBC-TV's "Silver Linings" (June 1987); and they appeared ensemble on the revived "Gong Show" (July 1988; now at CBS-TV). Pat was also a winner in the gospel category at the 1988 International Musical Saw Festival and Saw-Off.

During the summer of 1985, Pat went to Europe with her church choir, which performed in Switzerland, Germany, and Austria. She packed her new Mussehl & Westphal saw and a violin bow so she could exchange saw notes with Elfriede Hablé in Vienna. Says Pat, "Elfriede looks just like her picture, and she moves like a ballet dancer when she plays."

Patricia Graham, the Saw-C-Lady

Kathryn Fain does not play the saw, but she is close to someone who does, her mother, BEULAH TRACY BILLINGSLEY. "My step-father, Arthur Billingsley, taught Mama to play. He was a featured performer in the 1920s on the Grand Ol' Opry in Nashville's Reimann Auditorium. . . . But Mama had her own style, so they never dueted. In fact, she never played too much until he died [October 1977], then she picked it up again. She plays very mellow and soft. Arthur always played hard, loud and firm. He could make the saw say words."

As a fifth grader in 1975, JANEEN RAE HELLER of Burbank, California, heard Jim Turner play the saw with his band, at her elementary school. When he asked for a volunteer to come up and try playing the saw with a mallet, she eagerly raised her hand. "I already played the guitar by ear, so I was really excited to try the saw," Janeen says.

"That day after school I ran home and found an old rusty saw in the garage. I padded the handle of my hairbrush with tissue paper and tied it off with a rubber band. I succeeded in playing 'Twinkle, Twinkle Little Star.' I soon learned that I could play any melody I could sing."

For a year or so, Janeen continues, "I banged away on the saw, at the school playground, in talent contests, and at summer camp. It was always a source of excitement and fascination. Eventually, my father, aware of my musical interests, ordered a professional musical saw for me."

A couple of years after their first meeting in 1975, Janeen again met Jim Turner, this time in Denver, Colorado. "He was performing at a concert in a local park. I talked to him before he went on stage and later he asked me to come up out of the audience and play a tune. There were a few thousand people there, so I took no chances and played my fifth grade standard, 'Twinkle, Twinkle Little Star.'"

During high school Janeen was busy with other things and the saw came out only for special occasions. But during her first year as a student at Colorado University in Boulder, while working part-time as an entertainer at various restaurants and cocktail lounges, she added the musical saw to her guitar and singing act. It was about this time, she says, "that I met the players in the Blimping Blues Band and played with them whenever I could. It was an important evolution in my saw playing because I discovered what a wonderful blues instrument it is. Improvisation is my specialty and I played styles of music with the band that I never dreamed could be played on the saw."

Since leaving Colorado, Janeen has played frequently in Los Angeles and San Francisco, and counts among her credits engagements with bandmen Terry Wollman and Bill Whiteacre, and the Blues for Breakfast Band; and she played on 'The World Unseen' cut of "The Ghosters" album.

In competition, she placed first in the jazz category at the 1985 Festival of the Saws, in Portland, Oregon; and in 1987 she won second place in Pop-Jazz at the International Musical Saw Festival and Saw-Off, Northridge, California.

Janeen Heller, International Musical Saw Festival and Saw-Off, 1988 (Adam Leonard, photographer)

Dear Mr. Leonard:

I am sixty-seven years old, and when I was a little girl back in the 1920s I lived in Milwaukee, Wisconsin. My aunt would take me to see silent movies and vaudeville shows. Those were the days when the shows consisted of trained seals, xylophone players, tap dancers, whistlers, comedians and so forth. This is where I saw my first sawyer, a man by the name of Tom Scribner, if my memory is correct. I was so fascinated that my aunt let me stay for two performances. After that, whenever there was a sawyer, I made sure she took me. . . . I decided then and there that I wanted to be a saw player. Of course, everyone laughed at me, but I didn't think it was funny at all, and I cried when my mother made me learn the piano —never did do well with it, sorry to say.

In 1982, when I saw an ad in *Yankee Magazine* for a Mussehl & Westphal saw, I said to myself, This is the opportunity I've waited for all my life. I didn't tell my husband or four married children. Much to my dismay, when the saw came I couldn't get so much as a squeal out of it. The bow looked like it belonged to a kid's bow and arrow set, so I figured that's why I couldn't play it and told my husband I wanted a violin bow. "What do you want that for? You don't have a violin," he said. So I had to tell him about my saw. After much kidding, he said, "By golly with that much determination, maybe you can do it," and he located a bow that cost him $50.

. . . It was about five weeks before Christmas and I had made up my mind to play "Silent Night" for our family's annual party. Each year we put on a little show, and when it was my turn to entertain I excused myself saying I had to get my instrument. They knew I didn't play an instrument, so they all started to laugh. But when I came back into the room with my beloved saw, everybody literally came unglued. When I started to play, one of my grandchildren said, "Grandma's playing 'Silent Night,' " and my daughters had tears in their eyes. I played so well I even surprised myself! They wanted an encore, but that was the only song I knew how to play.

Sincerely,
JOAN F. SNYDER
Lancaster, California

PART III

Supersaw's Approach to Musical Sawing

Saws

I saw, you saw, we've all seen a C saw, an A-flat or an A-sharp saw. So what about saws? Musical saws, that is. To start with, your dad or grandpa most likely has one hanging in the garage or the wood shed. Surprisingly enough, many of these carpenter's saws work as a musical instrument. But unfortunately, as such, they don't play as well as one made especially for music.

Probably the first musical saw was one originally made for sawing wood. Let's imagine that one rainy day, while a carpenter sat around waiting for the rain to stop so he could go to work, his frustration got the better of him and he struck his saw with his hammer or a piece of firewood. And behold! A musical note came forth. Whoever this individual was —and he certainly didn't know it then —he started a movement that would sweep the world.

I've played many saws and I can hardly contain myself when I go into a store that sells tools. I always hedge over to the hardware section and promptly pull all the saws down and try them out. Everything from a $1.97 K-Mart to a $20 Sandvik. No two saws of the same model will sound alike or feel the same. I've gone through hundreds and they're all different.

There have been a number of companies over the years —some good, some better, and some just plain bad —that have produced saws for musical use. But only one, to my knowledge, has survived the test of time, and that's Mussehl & Westphal, the original professional musical saw company, now located in Delavan, Wisconsin.

Another oldie still in business is Sandvik Aktiebolag (Sandvik AB) in Sandviken, Sweden. Along with their regular line of carpenters' saws, they've manufactured the "Stradivarius" musical saw since the late 1920s.

In the beginning, the saw factory had a foreman, Ivar Fossell, who was a violinist, and he carried out a series of tests that finally resulted in the Sandvik 296 "Stradivarius" handsaw. Each one was tested by Fossell before being sent out. The old "Stradivarius" saws are very rare, and like the gold-plated Mussehl & Westphal, if you find one, grab it!

For more than a decade after the mid-1960s, Sandvik stopped manufacturing musical saws altogether. When I wrote to the company early in 1982, Ake Sundby (the Sandvik representative in the Saw and Tools Division) answered: "About 15 years ago we seem to have produced the latest batch of our 'Stradivarius' musical saws, which have lasted us up till now. The demand is obviously limited and musical saws seem to have a very long life. The volume does not justify production for commercial reasons, but we are contemplating to produce another batch to be able to respond to odd inquiries dropping in now and then from around the globe."

Later in 1982, the Sandvik company decided to continue the "Stradivarius" as part of their saw assortment and the company now puts out about 500 a year. Why so few? The problem, according to published company material, is that "the saw for playing is never worn out. The people use the wrong side of the blade. Sandvik 'Stradivarius' is no big product for us, but it gives Sandvik a good P.R. [public relations]."

Size and flexibility. Most musical saws run approximately 28 inches in length along the tooth side. The backside measurement will vary from handle to tip because of the tapered cut. The longest "Stradivarius" is 30 1/2 inches. The Mussehl & Westphal is close to a normal handsaw size in most dimensions: approximately 5 1/2 inches wide at the handle and 2 inches wide at the tip. This produces about a 2 1/2-octave range. By comparison, my two "Stradivarius" saws are 7 inches at the handle and 2 1/2 inches at the tip, giving them about a 3-octave range or better.

The thickness of the metal on the M & W is .040 inch (40/1000 of an inch), but on my prized gold saw that Dan Wallace gave me, the steel is .035 inch, which makes it more flexible and easier to play. (Later on I will explain this saw's modifications.)

Flexibility is a must for a musical saw, otherwise you can't bend it into the S curve for playing, and if it's too thick it will be very stiff and your fingers and wrist will tire quickly. Flexibility is also necessary to reach the tones at the high end of the scale. If you can't play at the tip end, you lose the higher register and eliminate the potential range of your saw.

Testing. Testing a saw for its tonal quality can be a drag, especially if you don't know how to play one and you decide to buy a hardware saw off the shelf. To test it properly you must play it and run the scale, or use the carpenters' old trick of snapping the saw to judge the steel's "temperament."

What's that? You don't know how to snap a saw? Hold it at both ends. With the teeth facing you, slip one hand through the handle slot so your thumb is on top. Grab the tip with your other hand, three fingers underneath and your thumb on top. Now, simultaneously, strike the metal at the base of the handle with your thumb while you "push" the two ends together and tweak the tip up at the same time, which makes an S curve. By quickly bending the blade from the tip while striking it with your thumb you can run up and down the scale to determine the saw's range. The longer it rings, the better, because the saw's ability to sustain notes is an important part of your playing. And notice the tone. Is it a dull sound or rich and pure? Do you hear continuous quality tone along the length of the saw?

Actually, although testing a saw can be fun, to save a lot of trouble, I recommend buying a professional saw because these folks have gone through a lot to produce the right one for you. Professional musical saws are usually made from imported steel that has been specially tempered for flexibility and response.

Care. Keep the bow and back edge of the saw absolutely clean of any foreign matter. Never wax or oil your saw. And NEVER put your fingers —and don't let anyone else put their pinkies —on the back edge of the saw where you apply the rosin and bow. Hand oils can be transferred from the blade to the bow and vice versa, and this will cause your bow to slip and not properly catch the saw blade. It's possible to lose vibration when this happens and you can end up with a dead spot in the tune you're playing.

To clean the blade, I use a soft cloth with Windex®, Formula 409®, or a non-creamy dishwashing liquid. Rinse thoroughly and wipe dry.

Modifying a Saw

I've discovered ways to alter a saw, if necessary, to increase the range. Originally, I modified the gold saw that Dan Wallace gave me, and later I applied the same changes to my "Stradivarius." A number of the sawyers included in this book have reported excellent results with the following modifications.

Shearing the blade. A local sheet metal shop can shear the back of the blade from the tip to the handle. Be careful with this modification, or you might ruin a good saw.

A normal saw is approximately 2 inches wide at the tip. I like mine about 1 1/4 inches wide. By cutting the extra metal off the back edge, you are able to:

- improve the saw's flexibility
- place the notes closer together
- increase the range by half an octave or more

Shearing the back edge actually allows you to play faster on up-tempo songs, yet it doesn't affect the quality of slower tempos. It's true that you lose some tone —minimal at worst —but I think the advantages of shearing a blade outweigh the slight loss of tone.

Squaring the edge. Next, I square the back edge. Saw manufacturers round the edge, which seems to work well with string bows, but since I use a cello bow, I find that a sharp, clean edge —like on ice skates —grabs the rosin and the bow better. I can achieve faster note response on bow contact.

To square the edge, I first clamp the saw in a vise with padded jaws (you don't want to scratch the finish). Then, using a flat file, I square the saw's edge so I have two 90-degree corners.

Handle. As to handle modifications, I've experimented with some and haven't found any advantage yet in changing the handle in any way, shape, or form.

Bows

Bows come in many assorted sizes and shapes. The choice between the type of hair or fiber that the bow is strung with also varies considerably, depending on what's to be played; whether it will be a fast or slow melody, or a recording, and so forth.

Black horsehair. A black horsehair bow is coarse and has more "bite" (better traction with the blade) than other types of hair or synthetic fibers. It's especially good for playing fast tunes that require rapid note changes, like "Tico Tico" or "Under the Double Eagle." When playing with a group of other instruments, a sawyer using a black horsehair bow will stand out considerably; although some people would say the saw has a habit of being conspicuous anyplace, even when it's buried in the midst of other instruments —sort of like a cat fight in the middle of a busy downtown intersection on a Saturday night!

White horsehair. For recordings and slower tempos, I use a white horsehair bow. The hairs are finer, softer, and the swishing sound it produces on contact with the saw's edge is almost undetectable and much lower in volume compared to the noisier whoosh that the black horsehair gives off. The amount of unpleasant noise you make with your bow is determined by how much you practice. The more time you're willing to spend, the fewer squeaks and buzzes you'll hear.

String bows. String bows (like those shipped with Mussehl & Westphal saws) are nearly as good and the closest you'll come to a real hair bow. They feel different on contact with the blade, but work very well, and with patience and —again —practice, they can be mastered. One advantage to the string bow is that it doesn't chirp or buzz like a horsehair bow.

Synthetic fibers. A bow can be strung with almost any kind of synthetic fiber, but I've found synthetics to be unsatisfactory compared to horsehair. First, synthetic fibers are too smooth and have no "bite." Second, the rosin doesn't stick very well and this affects your playing. Synthetic fibers are quieter than horsehair, though, making them good for recording, provided the microphone is placed close to the blade. The best way to test a bow's quality is to record your playing and listen to it. Then you'll hear what everyone else is hearing, good and bad.

Supersaw's druthers. My bows are custom made, with the hair cut slightly shorter so I can tighten the bow until it has a good bend in it, making the hair real taut. The amount of tension placed on a hair bow depends on the artist's preference. I like it super tight because I bow on the edge rather than on the flat side of the hairs. This decreases bow buzz. By bowing on the edge, only a few hairs are in contact with the saw, leaving the back hairs slack, which helps to muffle the unpleasant buzzing.

Flexibility. It's important to maintain the bow's flexibility, so always release the tension when you're not using your bow.

If the truth be known, a saw can be played with any object that you care to rub across the edge; everything from a yardstick to a pencil to a coat hanger to . . . you name it. Walk into a hardware store sometime, find a saw, pull off the plastic sheath covering the teeth and use it as a bow. You'll really surprise folks!

Cost. Bows can cost anywhere from $30 for a fiber glass bow to $4,000 for an ivory, cherry wood or diamond studded bow, if you're so inclined. However, an inexpensive bow from Sears works just great.

Length. I prefer a cello bow for its extra strength and length. If you have short arms, probably a short bow would be more comfortable to use, but the longer ones are preferable because they're more rugged and you get a longer stroke.

Care. For cleaning the bow, I use a clear dishwashing liquid (I find it cuts grease and oil better than a creamy soap), and gently wash the tightened hair. I'm especially careful not to get water in the frog (the gear box). Then I whip the bow through the air several times to throw out most of the water, and let it dry with the hair loose.

To remove old rosin and oily residue from the bow hairs, and to keep them from matting, clean the loosened hairs with shellac thinner and a cloth. Swish the bow to dry it. Don't get the thinner on the bow, or you'll ruin the finish. DO THIS OUTDOORS, AND AWAY FROM AN OPEN FLAME!

Rosin. Every time you play a piece, apply a good grade of rosin to the bow. I use bass bow rosin. It's versatile and works in hot or cold weather.

Rosin the bow in the same manner as a violinist would: Hold the rosin in one hand and the bow in the other. Quickly draw ONLY two or three inches of the bow across the rosin cake. After thoroughly rosining this spot, move on to the next two or three inches, applying the rosin on the top and bottom and along both sides. You want to rosin the entire bow because a long song will cause a loss of rosin on parts of the hair. When this happens you can roll the bow to the other side where the rosin is still heavy.

You rosin only two or three inches at once because sometimes a hair will hang up in a crack and snap off if you draw the whole bow across the cake. Horsehair is going for about $300 a pound now —need I say more?

It isn't necessary to remove the rosin that accumulates on the edge of the saw. It won't hurt anything and is better than none. But, if you must clean off the rosin, carefully scrape the blade with a knife.

A No-No. I don't recommend using your professional musical saw to cut wood. The early musical saws sported offset teeth and were sharp, but today's models are made of mild tempered steel that won't hold an edge, and the teeth aren't offset. The teeth on a professional saw are for show really, and to honor the musical saw's woodcutting predecessor. Also, the professional saws are lacquered to prevent rust and to protect the blade's design, which would be ruined if you attempt to cut wood.

I also suggest that you keep your saw and bow away from excessive humidity or heat. Otherwise, you'll have a gooey mess when the rosin begins to melt and all the bow hairs start matting together!

Sawing a Song

Folks, before I play
I'd like to say a word
About the seeing and the sawing
Of the saw that will be heard.

Both the saw and the bow I handle
Both belong to me
And when my hand is on the handle
The saw is all you see.

If you ever heard the saw I handle
Being sawed by me
You've seen the saw I saw
And you've heard the saw you see.

JEROLD S. MEYER
North Lima, Ohio

Seat Thyself. Find a comfortable straight-back chair without arms, or use a stool. Now, with your bow well rosined and your enthusiasm in overdrive to learn musical sawing, sit down and place the handle between your legs, with the teeth facing you. (If you're a "southsaw" reverse the following directions.) Your left foot should be flat on the floor. The right foot should be raised on the toes slightly and pulled back so the toes are almost even with your left heel (see illustration, Putting It All Together). This position (1) raises your right leg higher than the left, letting you get a firm grip on the saw handle; (2) provides the proper stance for the leg movement necessary for producing vibrato (more on that later).

Avoid touching the blade against either leg because this will reduce the saw's ability to vibrate.

Putting It All Together

Bending the saw. Grasp the tip end of the saw blade with your left hand. Place your thumb on the top side and your second, third (and sometimes fourth) fingers on the bottom. Slant the instrument at a 45-degree angle and press the handle into your right leg just behind your knee (not your upper thigh).

Helpful hint: I found that the handle pressing into my leg muscle was uncomfortable, and often the saw would slip down so I was nearly falling off my chair to bow the high notes. To remedy that, I wear non-slip clothing —usually corduroy pants — and drape a felt pad (any bulky, clingy material will do) across my lap with a "sling" hanging down between my knees to support the handle. Now I can sit in an upright position and the saw doesn't slip between my legs.

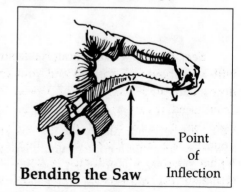

Bending the Saw — Point of Inflection

The secret of sawing music is the S or double curve that you put into the blade. As you bend the saw towards the floor, simultaneously press the thumb of your left hand into the saw (about two inches down the tip) and pull up on the saw's tip with your fingers. This action will give the saw a double curve.

Making the S curve may initially tire your fingers, but —here we go again! —with practice they'll get stronger. Just imagine what beautiful music you'll be making before too long!

Music, Maestro

Mallet. For the following instructions I'll concentrate on bowing the saw, but I recommend that you start with a felt-tipped mallet (like a tympani mallet, which you can purchase at a music store). Why? Because initially it's easier to hammer a saw and receive encouraging results in the form of a well-played scale or recognizable song —always a source of great satisfaction for the beginner. Also, using a mallet first will preserve your bow until you've gained some experience in knowing exactly where you want to attack the saw's edge to produce a tone.

With respect to the playing instructions below, you strike a saw with a mallet in the same place that you would bow it. The only difference is that you place the mallet on the flat surface of the blade, while the bow is positioned on the saw's back edge, hence the expression "scratch my back."

Bow. Hold the bow with your thumb on one side and your next three fingers on the other, about 2/3 of the way up the bow shaft.

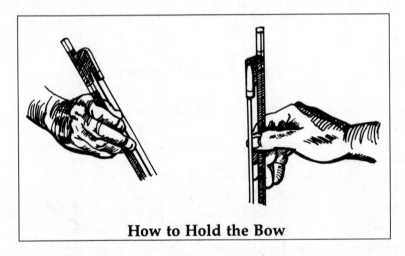

How to Hold the Bow

To make a note, draw the bow across the edge just above the top of the big curve. Keep the bow perpendicular to the floor as you stroke the saw (remember what Tom Scribner said: Saw on the smooth edge or you'll rip your bow all to hell!)

The speed with which you draw the bow across the saw, plus the proper amount of applied pressure, determine whether you'll produce a smooth tone or a series of chirps and squeaks. To prevent squeaking and to sustain the vibration during stroking, attempt to apply most of the bow pressure with the initial contact stroke. Once the saw is vibrating, the pressure is almost constant and must be continued to keep the metal alive. Don't expect to play perfectly in the beginning. You'll have weird sounds —or nothing at all —and that's okay until you get the knack of bowing.

Some sawyers stroke in only one direction —always up or always down. That's a lot of work, and often squeaky! I bow in both directions because this keeps the saw's vibration going and the tone is smoother. While another sawyer using a single-direction stroke is getting ready to attack the saw again, I'm already into my next note.

Buzz. A critical relationship —one I can't explain —seems to exist between the bowing speed and the particular note being played. If you are bowing too slowly, you may hear an unpleasant buzzing from the saw. This buzz, which is the result of an interaction between the blade and bow, is more conspicuous during the playing of low notes than high notes. Bow a little faster and the buzz should be significantly reduced.

Pitch. To reach the higher notes, bend the tip of the saw towards the floor. If you bend the saw upwards, the lower the pitch will be. Every time you change the pitch, you must bow at a different place, because you have changed the curvature of the blade.

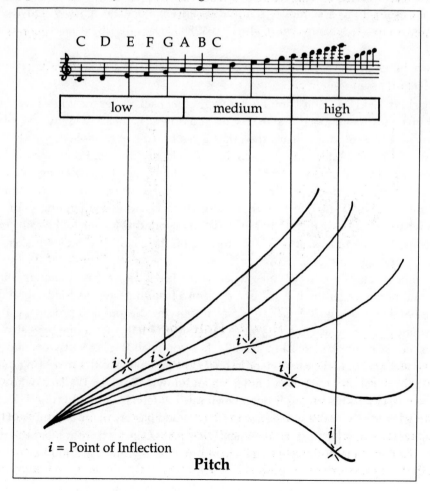

i = Point of Inflection

Pitch

For a high note, place the bow near the tip. For a low note, stroke near the handle. (Be sure the handle is held firmly just behind your knees because a change of position here will also affect the blade's curve.)

Practice reaching the low notes first because they're the hardest. Try to pick out the scale: do, re, mi, fa, sol, la, ti, do.

Once you have mastered the scale in the low and high registers, you can begin to sound out some of your favorite simple melodies ("Feelings" or "Home on the Range," for example). If you can practice with musical accompaniment, all the better. A piano-playing friend will help you pick out your notes more easily and you'll feel like a real performer. You may accomplish more in one evening together than you would on your own in a week.

DON'T get discouraged! You'll encounter problems, but play with the saw, have fun, and soon you'll experience a sawnsational improvement. Thirty minutes a day should do it for the first couple of weeks. If your fingers get tired, break up your practice sessions into shorter periods several times a day.

If you have questions, I'm always glad to help, and appreciate receiving letters, tapes, and photos. Please include a stamped, self-addressed envelope for a reply. My address: Jim Leonard, P.O. Box 2183, Santa Ana, California 92707.

Vibrato

As a child, I had the habit of pulling my right foot back under me while I was sitting, then raising it up on my toes and jiggling the leg up and down. I already had my saw vibrato down pat —now all I had to do was learn the other three-fourths of saw playing!

I was one of the lucky ones —or maybe I should say my neighbors were —because my learning period was a short one. It took me about an hour, then I was playing tunes on my saw to the accompaniment of a Wayne King record. Within a week, I was putting on shows.

Vibrato (the vibrating effect on the blade which is caused by jiggling your leg up and down) is what produces the feeling and expression in your music (much like using organ stops, or the pedals on a piano). Vibrato is the frosting on the cake. The cat's whiskers. It's what makes your saw sigh and cry.

To some extent, the saw vibrates when you slide a bow across the edge, but that isn't sufficient vibration to get the full volume of sound from the saw. Added vibration through movement of your leg or wrist has the effect of amplifying the tone and producing a continuous flow of sound waves, which enable you to carry several notes with one bow stroke. A little vibration should be applied at all times, whether you wish to play softly or loudly.

Most players jiggle their saw-handle-holding leg to achieve the trembling quality. I lay my saw to the left and bounce my right leg up and down. But Dan Wallace, who also laid his saw to the left, jiggled his left leg to achieve vibrato. A few, like my old friend, Tom Scribner, "shiver" the blade's tip with a wrist action. This method has saved me a number of times when I was nervous and my leg "froze," or when I was just plain tired from lots of playing. With practice, whether using your leg or wrist, you'll perfect a vibrato technique.

The Saw's Mysterious Musicality

The strange and beautiful sound of the musical saw is derived from the vibration of the saw blade. The nature of the vibration is extremely complex, and no one —to our knowledge —has successfully discovered the intricacies of the saw's musical sound.

In what follows, I describe the relationship between musical notes and the vibration of the blade, but I don't claim to fully understand the sound production of this remarkable instrument. The explanations and analogies are oversimplifications aimed at providing some basic ideas, and my experiments offer a technique which will allow readers an opportunity to explore on their own the nature of the saw's sound production.

Sound Production

A saw properly bent into an S curve will vibrate within a zone centered at the point where the player bows or strikes the blade. Although the sound for a given tone is derived mostly from vibrations which occur within this zone, the entire saw blade is involved in a complex way with every tone.

The blade's vibration within this zone is demonstrated in the cross section below. When the blade is attacked with a bow or mallet, the center (point C) moves up and down. When the center is up, the edges of the blade (points E) are down. When the center moves down, the edges move up. No

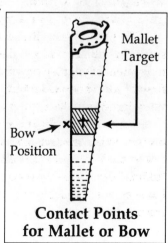

Contact Points for Mallet or Bow

movement occurs at the nodal lines (N).

Baby powder experiment. To investigate the source of the saw's sound, I conducted an experiment that allowed me to see the saw's areas of vibration and nodes (non-movement). After sprinkling baby powder on my Sandvik, I played "Stardust." The principle here is: The baby powder grains dance frantically and move away from areas where the blade is in motion, eventually coming to rest where the saw blade is not moving.

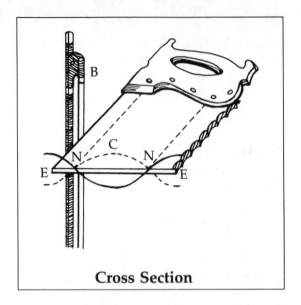

Cross Section

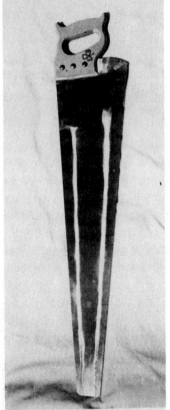

The saw's areas of vibration and nodes (non-movement; Jim Leonard, photographer)

In other words, in the photos you can observe how the powder has moved into two continuous nodal lines where the blade doesn't vibrate. The "clean" area is where the blade is in motion. It appears that the nodal lines get farther apart as the width of the blade increases. This is consistent with the fact that the lower tones (lower frequency or pitch) are played on the handle end, while the higher tones are associated with vibration zones at the tip end of the saw blade.

The broken line of powder beads in the blade's center suggests a complex nodal pattern that might be associated with my particular style for reaching notes in the lower register. But I honestly don't understand what happens here and consider this an excellent example of the difficulty in uncovering the complex elements of the saw's sound production.

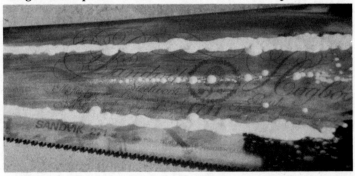

Formation of nodal lines and a complex nodal pattern, possibly in the saw's lower register (Jim Leonard, photographer)

Pencil test. The same experiment can be conducted using a pencil (which is less messy than the baby powder!). While the sawyer plays, another person can lightly touch the eraser tip to the blade and feel the vibrations as the pencil is moved from one edge to the other. When the eraser reaches a node you will not feel a vibration and the tone is not affected (i.e., the saw continues to sing). The singing saw stops, however, when the pencil arrives at a "live" (vibrating) area.

Music Production

As mentioned before, there are two steps involved in producing a particular musical tone on the saw:

      (1) The saw is bent into an S curve so the inflection point is at or very near
            the location (zone of vibration) which is associated with the desired tone

      (2) The saw is bowed or hammered at this location

Imagine a saw blade in terms of a piano keyboard, a xylophone, a harp, or similar instruments where high tones are played on one end and low tones are played on the other end, with a gradation of tones in between. I've made a direct analogy between the saw blade and the piano keyboard, and include a concept which involves a comparison with the harp and a set of simple wind chimes.

The concept. The low tones on the harp are played using the long strings. The low tones on a set of chimes are likewise heard when the longer chimes are put into motion. This concept is directly applicable to the musical saw. The wide portion of the saw near the handle can be made to vibrate with low-frequency tones, while the highest notes are played at the narrower end. The tonal span extending the length of the professional musical saw can exceed two octaves.

Piano analogy. Like the piano, where each key designates a certain pitch, a particular tone on the saw is related to a specific place. But a significant difference between the two instruments is the spacing between notes. In contrast to the piano keys' equal width, the saw exhibits a continuous change in the space between locations (zones of vibration) where consecutive tones are played. Near the handle or low-tone end, consecutive tones on the musical scale are widely spaced. The spacing becomes progressively smaller, however, toward the tip or high-tone end of the blade.

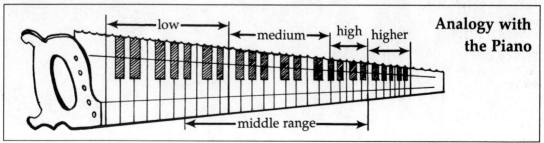

Analogy with the Piano

Each key on a piano corresponds to a distinct tone. But a saw —because it is constructed of a single sheet of metal without any individual "keys" —offers a spectrum of tones up and down the scale that can be equated with playing between the cracks of the piano keys.

Summary

Both the piano and the musical saw produce sound by generating a vibration. Each tone on a piano is clear and distinct because it is derived from a wire that is vibrating at a single frequency (pitch). The beautiful music that can be produced on the piano is due to the pianist's skill at combining these pure tones (a single frequency with harmonics) into harmonious patterns.

The saw's music, however, is quite different. In contrast to only eighty-eight tones such as the piano offers, the saw blade features an infinite number of locations where sound can be produced with a bow or a mallet. At each of these locations, the saw's sound is not the product of a single frequency, but rather it is a complex mingling of many frequencies. This union of multifrequencies is the basis for the rich and haunting music that can be delivered by a skilled sawyer.

A P P E N D I C E S

Appendix A

Saw Brands

During our research we came across the following brands of saws used by some of our contributors.

1- Arrow

2- Bear (circa 1930s, Alaska)

3- C. Blacklock Special

4- Disston

5- E.C. Atkins

6- Feldmann Singende Sage/Marke Jager (Germany)

7- Mussehl & Westphal Professional Musical Saw and the company's Broadcasting Model (circa 1920s)

8- Nicholson 300

9- Sandvik "Stradivarius" (Sweden)

10- Simonds Saw & Steel

11- Speliplari (Finland)

12- Stanley Handyman

13- Tyzack & Turner (Sheffield, England)

Appendix B

Saw Albums

The following recorded albums were collected during our correspondence with sawyers. Some feature the musical saw as a solo instrument (marked by an *); others include the saw as part of a musical ensemble. The albums are listed alphabetically, with the sawyer's name in parentheses.

- A Musical C-Saw* (Joe Hunter)
- Appalachian Dulcimer (Vicki Bolam)
- Blue Sky Serenaders (Joel Eckhaus)
- The Bluegrass Family Band (Gary Froiland)
- Concerto for Saw* (Robert C. Pritikin)
- Cranberry Lake (Joel Eckhaus)
- Die virtuose Sage* (Elfriede Hablé)
- He Cuts and Nails Notes* (McKinley A. DeShield, Jr.)
- I Will Praise Him* (Moses Josiah)
- Margaret Plays the Saw* (Margaret Steinbuch)
- Musical Saws* (Joe Hunter)
- Musical Saws (Clarence Mussehl; demonstration recording, no longer available)
- Old Time Favorites* (William L. Ormandy)
- One Flew Over the Cuckoo's Nest (original film soundtrack, Robert E. Armstrong)
- R. Crumb and his Cheap Suit Serenaders; albums #1, #2, and #3 (Robert E. Armstrong)
- Scratch My Back* (Jim Leonard)
- Songs of the Heartland (Art Thieme)
- Super Saw* (Jim Leonard)
- There's a Song in My Saw* (Robert C. Pritikin)
- Through It All* (Moses Josiah)
- Virtuoso Saw* (David Weiss)
- The Well-Tempered Saw* (Jim Turner)

Appendix C

To Cherished Friends Old and New

[Editor's note: Clyde Dawson "snuck around to the side of the Golden Gate" on November 11, 1984. But before leaving, he wrote a Christmas poem which we share with you.]

1984

```
Well, once again instead of cards, we send our thoughts in rhyme;
    A brief review of what we do...while we still have the time.
It seems like only yesterday that Santa Claus was here,
    I don't know where the time has gone...to end another year.

We had a thrilling ride in June aboard the Freedom Train,
    On its return from New Orleans...to never run again.
It was the part of history  once called the Age of Steam,
    And it brought miles of memories...like being in a dream.

There was another scenic tour aboard the Vera Cruz,
    New York to Bonaventure...Fantastic shoreline views.
Nova Scotia back to Montreal was only half the fun,
    That makes a trip you won't forget...long after it is done.

The first day you are out to sea you start with Planters Punch,
    That's with your hotcake and an egg...Screwdrivers are for lunch!
At  three o'clock it's Rum and Coke, that's called the Happy Hour,
    At dinner with your T-bone steak...you get a whiskey Sour!

        These sentimental journeys left this one thought with me
        That I had traveled back in time...the way life used to be.

Don and Carole were both here, we all had lots of fun;
    He lives in Arizona yet...and she's in Oregon.
To use some of our spare time, we still play with three bands,
    Making music with our friends...keeps time off our hands.

We watch the mirror on the wall to find a birthday wrinkle.
    And look for symptoms of old age..,like eyes that lose their twinkle.
So let's forget the old age blues  and start each day anew;
    Remember to "be young at heart"...and let that youth shine through.

        And thus ends one more span of time  we call another year.
        And here's a wish to all our friends who live both far and near.

        HEALTH AND HAPPINESS    Love, *Clyde & Louise*
```

Postscript: For my Dad with love...his daughter

This poem that my Daddy wrote for 1984
    Will be the last one you receive, there won't be anymore.
His earthly music won't be heard, except within our minds.
    But I believe he'll always play, and always create rhymes.

And though he reminisced of times when trains were powered by steam,
    Windmills pumped water, California air was clean,
The things that made him happy, and kept him "young at heart,"
    Can be summed up in his own words: "Each day's a brand new start."

And I just hope as years go by, you, his friends, recall
    The pleasures that he shared with you - he'd like that best of all.

Appendix D

Gary Mandell

Gary Mandell is an arranger-orchestrator who lives in Los Angeles. He teaches guitar at McCabe's Guitar Shop and Concert Hall in Santa Monica, where he also produces a monthly "Variety Night."

Mandell was commissioned by the Los Angeles Philharmonic to arrange the *American Music Medley* for the musical saw and orchestra. He scored the work for conventional symphony orchestra instruments and the piano, and added arrangements for the guitar. The medley was performed for the first time in 1985, at the Hollywood Bowl, featuring the Los Angeles Philharmonic and sawyer David Weiss.

In his orchestration of the medley —which includes songs by Stephen Foster, George Gershwin, Dan Emmet, and Erroll Garner —Mandell employed such strongly contrasting styles as country and impressionism, and he updated certain harmonies with contemporary chord combinations.

An accomplished pianist and guitarist, Mandell began arranging and producing jingles for radio and television in 1970. At that time he also began scoring for films and producing records. Mandell's credits include the arrangements for David Weiss's appearances on Johnny Carson's "Tonight Show."

Gary Mandell, arranger-orchestrator

Appendix E

The Winning Edge, or How to Compete Successfully in a Musical Saw Competition, by David Weiss

Playing the saw is quite unlike playing any other musical instrument. For one thing, there are not very many of us, and we're mostly self-taught. For another, to our audiences we appear more like magicians than musicians, because we are able to coax melodies out of our carpenters' tools. Audiences love us, even if we are barely able to play a recognizable tune. People can't believe their ears and often ask, "Aren't you really whistling?"

So, with all this individual attention —and believing we will dazzle everyone and walk away with a prize —off we go to our first musical saw competition. But for many of us it's the first time we ever encounter other sawyers, all with different styles and techniques, and some of them play very well. To our dismay we go from being a big fish in a small pond to being a smaller fish in a much bigger pond!

What, then, must we do to be a successful musical saw competitor?

HAVE THE RIGHT ATTITUDE

The saw festival should be looked upon as an enjoyable *learning* experience. Go with the attitude of absorbing as much information as possible. Look for what is good in each saw player's style, and don't be afraid to try new techniques.

Attend the workshops of the master sawyers. Learning just one or two little pointers from them can sometimes significantly improve your playing. In other words, learn from the contest itself. See how you deal with the stress of performing in front of your peers. You will discover strengths and weaknesses in your playing that you may never have noticed before and be able to use this knowledge to much better advantage in the next contest.

The judges are usually happy to critique your performance, and often a recording is made of the contest so that later, more objectively, you can evaluate your playing. If you win a prize, think of it as a bonus. But remember, even without a prize you can be extremely successful.

WHAT THE JUDGES LOOK FOR

Remember that playing the saw is both a musical and a visual experience. The first thing the judges look for is your overall presentation. The way you walk on stage and introduce yourself are very important. Are you confident, poised, getting the audience's attention in a positive way? What are you saying about your act? How are you projecting your stage manner? Good communication with the audience —both verbally and non-verbally —is the key here.

MUSIC SELECTIONS

Next is your choice of music. Pick tunes that display your abilities well without being too hard or too easy. It's usually a good bet to select familiar, likeable songs. Keep in mind that you want to demonstrate to the judges that you are able to play softly and loudly, with all the musical shadings in between.

A sense of musicality with respect to your choice of music is important. Do you play with feeling; keep a steady tempo and the right rhythm; and play the piece with the right style?

It's a good idea to tape yourself and play it for a few friends, to get their opinions. Are you playing too slow or too fast? Does the melody sound too difficult for your ability? Listen to a tape playback and try to concentrate objectively on your musical strengths and weaknesses.

PLAY ON PITCH

Also, can you stay on pitch? Playing in tune is especially important in saw playing. After all, we have no keys or frets or anything else, other than our own ears, to guide us. Being able to stay on pitch is the truest and most objective test of a good saw player. Again, to help you improve quickly, tape your own saw playing, perhaps with the accompaniment of a piano, then listen carefully to how well you maintain good pitch.

BOWING

Bow technique is another area of judging. Does the sound respond readily at the touch of the bow, or does it come late, or not at all? Learning the exact "sweet spot" where the bow contacts the saw is the secret to achieving a good musical response. This skill comes only with disciplined practice.

Check: Does your bow make scratchy noises on the saw edge or does it sound fairly pure? Can you bow up and down strokes? (Faster tunes may require that you bow both ways, although some sawyers are able to play fast by stroking only in one direction.)

There are also sawyers who put a little "bounce" in the bow, which helps to articulate single notes in a melody. Others use the palm of the hand to stop the continuous ringing sound that the saw makes. Also, by altering the pressure of the bow on the saw you can change the volume level quite a bit.

VIBRATO

What about vibrato? Can you control it? It isn't important how you get it, whether by jiggling the left or right leg, or by flexing the wrist. What is important is that it enhances the music. Don't vibrate so much that it becomes distracting. Remember, good saw playing is no longer the gimmicky sound-effects joke it once was. (The exception, however, is if sound effects are part of your novelty act, if you enter that category.)

Last, but definitely not least, if you go to a saw festival with the attitude of having a good time and learning something, you will be a winner —prize or no prize.

[Editor's note: To prepare for musical saw competitions, it is a good idea to listen to a few recordings of other sawyers; see Appendix B. The following saw players can provide information on their albums and possibly provide additional contacts. Enclosing a self-addressed stamped envelope would be appreciated.]

Moses Josiah	David Weiss	Jim Leonard
640 Hopkinson Avenue	Cut Time Records	Seada Records
Brooklyn, NY 11212	P.O. Box 64361	P.O. Box 2183
	Los Angeles, CA 90064	Santa Ana, CA 92707

About the Authors

Jim Leonard is a gas appliance repairman from Santa Ana, California, whose unprecedented fast-paced renditions of "Tico Tico" and "Twelfth Street Rag" at the 1979 Santa Cruz Saw Festival blew some folks' minds. Old-time sawyers had said only ballads and lullabyes could be played on the musical saw. Yelling out "The Supersaw!" the audience gave him a standing ovation, and the nickname stuck.

Leonard's first album, "Super Saw" (which he spent more than 800 hours perfecting in his home studio), reinforced his saw virtuosity and contributed to revolutionizing the art of musical sawing. In 1980 "Super Saw" was placed in Washington, D.C.'s Library of Congress and the Smithsonian Institution. His latest albums are "Scratch My Back" and "Cookbook."

Leonard performs regularly as a solo sawyer or with musical groups; at fairs, festivals, and such Southern California attractions as Disneyland and Magic Mountain. He appears fre-

quently on radio and television; performed in a music video with the rock group "Kansas"; appeared on KNBC-TV's "Silver Linings," with Christopher Nance, and on CBS-TV's "The Morning Program," with Mariette Hartley and Rolland Smith. His TV debut occurred in April 1976, when he was a contestant on the first "Gong Show." In July 1988, when the show was revived by CBS-TV, he was invited again to appear on the first program. Leonard organized the Sawyers Association Worldwide in 1985, and in 1987 started the annual International Musical Saw Festival and Saw-Off.

A man who does not read notes, but who improvises on several musical instruments, Leonard has devoted every spare moment since 1975 to promoting the musical saw and to improving his sawing technique. The results, he says, "are a far cry from the day I started sawing and chased the family —and a few dogs —into the hills."

Janet E. Graebner is a professional business writer and communications consultant working in areas as diverse as finance, oil, technology, veterinary medicine, real estate development, and . . . the musical saw. She met Jim Leonard when he asked her to design and write a brochure for his gas appliance repair business. He mentioned that he had "this book I want to write," and so began their collaboration on *Scratch My Back*.

Graebner's publishing credits include articles in regional and national publications: Christian Science Monitor, Los Angeles Times, California Business, The Executive, Electronic Business, Computer Merchandising, and others. Her first book, *Orange County: An Economic Celebration*, was published by Windsor Publications in 1988.

Since 1977 she and her husband, Peter, have lived in Santa Ana, California.

Ballard, Claude N. (known as Jed Sawyer). *The Musical Saw and How to Play It.* New York: Belwin, 1938 (Contributed by Ernest Peisker).

Bloomer, Frank J. "Music from a Carpenter's Saw." *The Etude,* July 1939 (Contributed by Ernest Peisker).

Bristol, Marc. "Homegrown Music and the Festival of the Saws." *The Mother Earth News,* pages 166-167, January/February 1980 (Contributed by Ernest Peisker).

Cioffi, Mickey. "Wisconsin Pilot Sells Saws That Sing." GRIT, May 10, 1981.

Fixmer, Rob. "For 59 Years, He Sang a Song of Saws." *Capital Times,* August 18, 1978.

Fletcher, Lucille. "The Apotheosis of the Handsaw." *The New Yorker,* pages 55-56, May 7, 1938 (Contributed by Ernest Peisker).

Foushee, Sandra. "Hark to the Sound of Sawing." Americana, page 112, September 1978.

Harris, Lillian E. "A Musical Heritage." Westways, pages 31-33, August 1984 (Contributed by Suzy Ingram).

Hillinger, Charles. "Pilot Goes for Music with Cutting Edge." *Los Angeles Times*,
     September 23, 1981.

Hughes, Michael. "The Blue Sky Serenaders Re-Living the Age of Croon."
     Sweet Potato, Vol. 8, No. 5, April 27-May 11, 1983.

Keller, Jacques. *La Lame sonore*. Paris: Henry LeMoine et Cie., 1950
     (Contributed by David Weiss).

Krier, Beth Ann. "A Saw Festival with Some Teeth in It." *Los Angeles Times*,
     September 9, 1981.

Runzler, Michael. "His is a Stradivarius of the Unusual Sort."
     The Orange County Register, November 3, 1983.

Shulgold, Marc. "He Came, He Sawed and He Conquered." *Los Angeles Times*,
     February 25, 1983.

Skretvedt, Randy. "It's a Bird . . . It's a Plane . . . It's Supersaw!"
     The Bluegrass Alternative, Vol. 1, No. 7, March 1981 (Contributed by Burney Garelick).

(Unattributed). "PhiloSAWphical Discourse on the Occasion of the
     4th Annual Festival of Saws." *The Bluegrass Alternative and The National Fiddler*,
     pages 32-35, August 1982 (Contributed by Burney Garelick).

Wallace, Dan. "More Than Just an Old Saw." *North Country Folk*, pages 24-27,
     March 1981 (Contribute by Burney Garelick).

Wilck, David G. "The New Vaudeville —Rebirth of a Family Entertainment."
     The Christian Science Monitor, September 13, 1982.